Take the Step,
the Bridge Will Be There

Rhian—
You are
perfect—
a Goddess!

Grace

We can easily forgive a child who is afraid of the dark.
The real tragedy of life is when men are afraid of the light.
—Plato

The average person does not know what to do with her life,
yet wants another one which will last forever.
—Anatole France

Grace Cirocco

Take the Step,
the Bridge Will Be There

XEPHOR
P R E S S

XEPHOR
P R E S S

Xephor Press
3 Holly Hill Lane
Katonah, NY 10536
www.xephorpress.com
914-232-6708

Cover Design: Greg Tabor
Author Photo: Glamour Shots

First United States edition

ISBN: 0-9752638-4-6

Printed and bound in the United States of America

For my mother, Concetta Cirocco
whose compassionate heart taught me faith.

For my father, Matteo Cirocco
whose courageous spirit taught me action.

And for Santo, Jasper and Kajsa
who teach me faith and action every day.

Contents

Acknowledgments

I am the person I am today because of the people who have loved me. I would like to celebrate and thank them for helping me become a fuller version of myself.

First to my parents, Matteo and Concetta Cirocco, who gave me life and who always gave me bigger shoes to wear. Their confidence and belief in me made me want to climb to higher peaks. *Grazie per tutto che avete fatto per me. Vi voglio bene.*

To my brothers John and Tony, with whom I share a name, a heritage, and precious memories, and their wives Aleksandra and Lori. Thank you for the privilege of being your sister. I love you and your wonderful children—Cassandra, Mathieu, Erika, and Kylie.

To Nonna Antonia and Nonno Emilio, who are on the "other side" now, but who continue to watch over me—your love and kindness was the purest I'll ever know. I am who I am because of you.

To my aunts, uncles, and cousins in Australia, France, and Italy. Thank you for welcoming me with open arms and for always showering me with love.

To my husband's brother and sisters and especially his mother, Lucy D'Agostino, thank you for your love and support.

Brian Weiss says friends make up our spiritual family. I am particularly blessed with a large spiritual family. I would like to acknowledge and celebrate you all:

Thanks to Caroline Cobham—for twenty years of friendship. Thanks, Care, for always wanting to celebrate my success and for coaching me with the phone call that made it all happen.

Thanks to Catherine Hurley, my soul sister, for her tail-wagging support over the years and for sharing nature's mysteries with me.

Thanks to Addie Greco-Sanchez, "Bella," for her infectious good humor, and her "phenomenal" support, especially while I was writing.

Thanks to Katalin Eszterhai for her pure heart, her friendship and her unconditional belief in me.

Thanks to Wally Morgado for being my number one fan. Your friendship continues to nourish me.

Thanks to John McCormick for his "wondrous" spirit, and for constantly blowing wind beneath my wings.

I also wish to thank the following people whose friendship and love have been a blessing: Nesrin Berrak, Leslie Chambers, Annika Daley, Lara D'Avilar, Tina DiPietro, B Doyle, Rosemary French, Ellen Goldhar, Joanne Harrington, Jill Hewlett, "Kris", George Lajtai, Jeanne Ma, D'Arcy MacKenzie, Linda Montgomery, Trisha Naylor, Nick and Gloria Olenick, Erick Sanchez, Sue Sheldon, Mary & Jim Slominski, Fatih Tinaz, Owen Williams, and Sara Yashar. All of you have been magical threads on my tapestry woven as part of my spiritual family in this lifetime. Thank you.

Thank you to Assistants, Barb Marks and Leah Taylor, I so appreciate your professionalism and dedication and gratitude goes to my incredible web designer and graphic artist, Angela Brooks and her team.

A special thank you to Neale Donald Walsch, Wayne Dyer, Blaine Lee, Brian Tracy, and Daphne Rose Kingma for their kind endorsements of my book and for inspiring me.

I am grateful to my clients, especially my "Goddesses" who have let me into their hearts and whose generous feedback over the years has fueled my faith to stay true to my calling. Thanks also to the thousands of people in the United States, Canada, Australia, and the United Kingdom who attended my workshops, seminars, and presentations and who shared their thoughts and feelings with me. Ultimately, it is the Divine Voice expressing itself to you through me that I credit for the courage to take the step and write this book.

To the many leaders who have hired me to lead workshops, or give keynotes, I thank you for the privilege of being able to serve you. You are the brave hearts our world needs today.

I am grateful to Dawn McKinney Maxwell at Fred Pryor Seminars in Kansas City, who was the first to recognize and celebrate my speaking gift.

This book was first published in Canada, and I would like to acknowledge and thank my editor, Don Loney at Harper Collins Canada, who was the first person to believe in my vision. Thanks also to the rest of the HarperCollins family who continue to support me.

Gratitude goes to Morty Mint who led me to Tom Woll at Xephor Press in the United States. Thanks to Tom. Thanks too to Xephor Press itself, whose mission is to bring inspiration and wellness to work and daily living. Gratitude also goes to the Marketing and Promotions Manager, MG McClelen whose infectious positive attitude is a blessing.

I could not have done this work without the love and support of my family. To my two precious children, Jasper and Kajsa. Your energy and passion for life inspire me. Your innocence renews me, and your love completes me. Thank you for choosing me as your mother and for constantly teaching me to take the step.

To my life partner, editor, and best friend, Santo D'Agostino. Your love is the rock I hold onto in the storm and the wind that carries me to seek higher versions of myself. I feel blessed that our stories intertwined in this lifetime. Everything makes sense because you're in the world.

And last, but not least, I want to acknowledge the Great Spirit that speaks through me, and allows me to do this work with so much passion and joy. As William Blake said, "I myself do nothing. The Holy Spirit accomplishes all through me."

Introduction

I was supposed to scale a vertical wall. It was smooth, shiny, and hard. It was made of black marble and went straight up. Climb this with my bare hands? Impossible, I thought, but I knew that at least one other person had done it, a Chinese acrobat. She was tiny and athletic. I had to get up the wall because I had to solve a computer problem of national importance on the other side. I was the only one who had the answer to the problem, yet I couldn't get over that darn wall. I tried and tried. Each time I slid right down to the bottom. There was nothing to hold on to.

"This is impossible," I thought, a bit annoyed. "It must be some sort of trick." I made all sorts of excuses why I couldn't do it. "I don't have the right body type. I'm not strong enough. Besides, I know nothing about computers." This went on for some time. Then I got tired of all the excuses. Some deep part of me knew that if I really wanted to, I could climb that slippery surface. But how? I had never done anything like that before.

I closed my eyes, took a deep breath, and said to myself, "I can do this." I began to repeat, "I can do it, I can do it, I can do it," over and over again to myself until it became a mantra. All the while, I was focusing on the marble wall. And then eight words appeared out of nowhere. *Take the step—the bridge will be there.* The words were there at the top of wall, beckoning me to go up.

"Take the step . . . Okay. The bridge will be there? What bridge?" There was no bridge. Just a wall. I needed to go over that wall. Okay, relax. Take a deep breath. Focus. Visualize. "Grace, you can do it! Grace, you can do it! *Just do it!*"

I opened my eyes—miraculously, I had climbed the wall. I was at the top. All I could think was, "Gee, was that ever easy!" I was exhilarated for a moment. "Wow, I did it!" And then the doubt came. "Yes, but could I do it again?" I needed to know, so I slid back down the wall. That was a risk!

I closed my eyes and saw the same eight words: *Take the step—the bridge will be there.* "Okay, I get it. *Do it with faith!*" Then I was climbing again, except this time it was even easier. I began thinking, "Maybe I should tell others about this."

Then I woke up.

Two years before I had that dream, I had left a secure, well-paying job to start my own training and consulting company. That was in the early 1990s; everywhere I looked, organizations were restructuring and re-engineering—and laying people off. Nobody wanted to hire an unknown when huge training companies with proven records were competing for work. With two toddlers, mounting debts, and a husband who also freelanced, I felt I could no longer afford to pay someone to watch my children while I went to my office to stare at the telephone. After two years of spinning my wheels, I made the decision to give up the call of my soul and get a "real" job.

And that's when I had the dream. Sometimes our souls send us messages just as we're about to turn our backs on our true path. That dream inspired me. It helped me believe in myself again. I wrote *Take the step—the bridge will be there* in huge black letters and stuck the paper on my office wall. Those words became my compass whenever I felt lost. They gave me courage to keep following my heart's desire and stay true to my soul's calling. Eventually, I designed a workshop called "Take the Step—The Bridge Will Be There," and over the past twelve years, I have helped tens of thousands of people take that step toward their dreams.

Action ("take the step") and faith ("the bridge will be there") are the two most important ingredients for achieving anything you want in your life. Typically, the problem is that if we want to take action, we don't move forward because we don't believe in ourselves. Or if we do believe in our abilities, we're too afraid to act. Rarely do we display both faith and action at the same time and in the right mix.

TAKING ACTION

My soul does not find itself unless it acts. Therefore, it must act. Stagnation and inactivity bring spiritual death.
—THOMAS MERTON

There are people who have plenty of faith, or so it would seem. They say they believe in themselves; they claim they can do anything. They appear confident and self-assured, and they talk constantly about all the things they're going to do—someday. These people can't move their lives forward because they don't move their feet. They procrastinate, they complain, they postpone their lives. They suffer from analysis paralysis. These people will, unfortunately, never know whether their faith is real or not because they never test it by taking action. The truth is you will never know whether you can really do something until you actually do it. Faith without action is not really faith. Only action makes faith real.

It is said that knowledge is power, but knowledge that lies dormant in your brain will not move your life forward. It's what you do with what you know that will make the difference in your life. The moment your brain sends the message, "Move" to your feet or "Speak" to your mouth is the moment when you walk across the bridge and change your life forever. What will it take for you to finally take the step?

People don't take action because they don't know what to do, where to go, or with whom to speak to, in short, they lack clarity about who they are. In the first three chapters of this book, you'll have an opportunity to grow your relationship with yourself. You'll be challenged with thought-provoking questions such as: "Who am I? What are my authentic gifts? What is my purpose? What makes my heart sing?" These chapters will help you dig for your truth, uncover what is sacred to you, and clarify the vision of your life.

NURTURING FAITH

> At your most daring moments you believe that what is going on is the ultimate human work—the shaping of a soul. The power of life comes from within; go there; pray; meditate. Reach for those luminous places in your Self.
>
> —ARDIS WHITMAN

On the other side of the coin are the "action heroes"—people who are risk takers, who have no trouble taking the step. On the outside, they appear to be fearless, dynamic, and in control. They have lots of projects on the go, but on the inside, they conceal doubts and fear. Their bridge of confidence is shaky. They can't move forward, because they don't have the necessary faith in themselves. They don't really believe they can be successful. They lack the connection to their magnificence. That is what happened to me. I took action—I registered a business, rented office space, and sent out hundreds of packages outlining my services. But deep down, I didn't really believe I could make a living from doing work that I loved.

Even though we're taking action on the outside, on the inside we may feel like imposters. Doubts, fears, and demons from the past rear their ugly heads. We lack the internal authority to silence the doubt and say, "Yes, this is possible. I can do it!" Consequently, the action we take is often miscalculated, off target, or not effective. Our body can't go to where our mind has never been. What we need to do first is convince ourselves that we *can* do it, visualize the outcome, and have the faith; *then* take the step.

In chapters 4, 5, and 6, I discuss ways you can heal your past, esteem yourself, and activate your courage. Many of us feel we can't cross the bridge because we don't have the right credentials or the proper background. We think that we may be "too much" or not enough. We believed the naysayers when they said, "It's too difficult" or "It's never been done before." Why would we challenge all those years of programmed beliefs? The path of least resistance is to believe what we're told. It's never what you *are* that holds you back—it's what you *think* you're not. That's why we need to grow our faith in ourselves if we are to achieve our goals. We need to make our bridge strong.

When I speak about "faith," I mean the faith we need to believe in our gifts, our talents, our dreams, our desires and our highest purpose. The amazing truth is that our belief in our ability is one hundred times more powerful than our ability. We've always suspected this to be true, but now recent research in cell

biology and quantum physics is confirming what spiritual masters have known all along—you must believe it (have the faith)
to achieve it. Our beliefs come from our past, our culture and
our environment. They are largely responsible for your success
and happiness. If you haven't been able to take the step with the
belief that your success is inevitable, then you probably haven't
reached your full potential.

Your bridge represents the quality of your faith—faith in your
dreams, in yourself, and in a divine Voice that whispers guidance to you and sustains you during periods of doubt. This faith
is like the tides; it is not always constant. There are days when
you feel you can slay any dragon, and other days when you
might as well offer yourself up as the dragon's next meal. The
only way to keep your faith strong is to turn within. You are a
fragment of the Divine Intelligence. On days when you feel disconnected from your purpose, or feel the fear rising, close your
eyes and go within. See your Light, connect to your Spirit, and
listen to the wisdom of your heart.

THE SPIRITUAL JOURNEY

The conditions of a solitary bird are five:
the first, that it flies to the highest point;
the second, that it does not suffer for company,
not even of its own kind;
the third, that it aims its beak to the skies;
the fourth, that it does not have a definite color;
the fifth, that it sings very softly.
—SAN JUAN DE LA CRUZ

There is a spiritual awakening happening on the planet. All
sorts of people who would otherwise not be open to a spiritual

dialogue are now having meaningful conversations. Perhaps the reason so many of us are thirsting for spiritual nourishment is because of the relentless change we've endured. In an effort to awaken to the beauty in our lives, we have embarked on a spiritual journey, a journey that has taken us through the dark nights of the soul and the fires of transformation.

The journey may be difficult and messy. Our fears can seem insurmountable, and as we attempt to cross the bridge, we can come face to face with the demons of the past. "Go back!" they shout. "The chasm will swallow you whole," they warn, but we press on. We take the step—and with each step we grow our souls. And as we cross the bridge, Spirit helps us welcome miracles into our lives.

Miracles happen when we believe in our magnificence and take the step toward meaningful action. Miracles take place when compassion envelops our hearts, and we see more clearly how to forgive and let go. Miracles follow us when we recognize the endless possibilities we have to create for ourselves. Miracles are everywhere when we truly believe that we're One and that healing the planet will begin with healing ourselves. We are finally blessed by miracles when we make peace with the divine Presence in our lives.

My hope is that the following pages will inspire you to cross the bridge to whatever future you desire. Once you're inspired, you'll have more confidence and courage to take bold steps. The answers are inside you; sometimes all you need to bring them forth are the right questions. May the reflections, personal stories, inspirational poems, quotations, suggestions, and practical exercises I've included in this book trigger the right questions for your spiritual journey.

As you're reading, let your mind meander to your life. Pause to reflect and jot down ideas that speak to you. Ask yourself,

"How does this apply to my life?" Ideas are like seeds. They are the raw material on which our bridges are built. When we nurture the seeds of faith, we realize we can do anything—even climb smooth vertical walls.

Faith and action are like two wings of an airplane that keep your life in flight. If only one wing works, your voyage may be turbulent. You will not get to your final destination. You may not even make a safe landing. If you want to move your life forward, you need to make the journey with both wings. "Take the step—the bridge will be there" could easily be, "The bridge is there, so take the step." It doesn't matter which part of the equation you work on first. You need faith *plus* action if you are to actualize the best version of yourself.

I was concluding a number of seminars in Australia when a young woman from Melbourne hugged me hard and whispered in my ear, "Thank you, Grace. You've changed my life." A month later I received a postcard from her saying, "You know when I whispered in your ear that *you* had changed my life? Well, I want you to know that you inspired me, but *I* changed my life. I didn't know that then, but I know that now and I wanted to share it with you." She had figured out the secret to her own empowerment.

Books, people, and resources can be rays of sunshine in your life, but remember, you are the sun. You are a unique work of art in progress. Every day your choices help create your masterpiece. Savor the journey. Belong to this world and shine.

GRACE CIROCCO
JUNE 2005

1

Honor Your Authentic Self

WHO AM I?

**Truth is within ourselves, it takes no rise
from outward things, whatever you may believe . . .**
—ROBERT BROWNING

I was riveted to the car radio, listening to Sister Anna Soloman, an Ojibway, tell her story. When she was fifteen, she was called to the bedside of her uncle, who had been hospitalized after being badly beaten by his friends. While sitting next to him, feeling both angry and sad, she asked God in desperation, "Why do native people beat each other up?" And then, like a flash, came the insight that would change the course of her life. "It's not alcohol," she thought. *"It's because they don't know who they are."*

When we feel alienated from the Self, we are disconnected from our Spirit. We've lost the key to our magnificence. We no longer feel like the unique miracles that we are. We are estranged from our core, authentic selves. Anna Soloman has spent her adult life helping aboriginal people reconnect with who they are and deal with this problem of self-alienation.

"Who am I?" is the central question facing every human being, and it is at the root of our spiritual quest. We must ask it again and again in order to begin our inner dialogue. This question will lead us on a conscious journey—the way out of self-alienation. This is how we can reconnect with our authentic selves. This is the way home.

STOPPING YOUR LIFE

**All of humanity's problems stem from man's
inability to sit quietly in a room alone.**
—BLAISE PASCAL

Who we are is not our jobs, our bodies, our families, our bank accounts, our cars, or any other material object. Who we are is not even the roles we play for others—mother, father, teacher, wife, neighbor, business person, manager, friend. Who we are transcends this world. Who we are is Spirit, Light, Love. How do we connect to this part of us in our crazy, fast-paced world?

Have you ever wondered what would happen if suddenly one day you just stopped your life? You know, as if someone had hit the "stop" button on an assembly line and everything came to a screeching halt. Have you ever wanted to take your Spirit on a holiday—just you and your Spirit? Have you ever wanted to take time out to just *be*?

I love watching people in busy urban centers, train stations, shopping malls, or just on the street, walking briskly to the next destination. I've always wanted to pretend I am some sort of pollster, so that I could stop some of them and ask them where they are going. "Excuse me, sir, I'm from the ABC Company.

We're doing a poll this evening. We want to know where people are going. Could you please tell us in your own words where you're off to at this precise moment?"

I'll bet I know what they would say: "I'm going home," or "I'm going to work" or "to see a movie" or "to meet a friend for dinner" or "to the gym" or "to the baby-sitter's" or "out for a walk." No one would look me in the eye and say, "Gee, I don't know . . . I'm taking my Spirit on a holiday to just *be*." We've all got such busy lives. We squeeze so much in. We're modern-day warriors pounding the pavement in the name of progress and economic growth. I marvel these days when I see people in airports linking themselves electronically to their offices via cell phone and e-mail. They're always trying to get in some last bit of business before boarding their planes. Most people are busy "going somewhere," their lives moving along at sometimes frightening speeds.

So what if you *could* stop your life? What if you had the luxury to step outside yourself and ask your authentic Self a few key questions—questions that would put your life into perspective? *Who am I? What do I really want? How do I want to belong in this world? Am I living an authentic life?*

Thousands of people asked themselves these questions during this past decade, when they were restructured out of jobs and pushed off the precipice, with no safety net below. When they landed, they had to pick up the pieces of their shattered worlds. Some, like Mark Albion, decided to catch up with their lives. In his book *Making a Life, Making a Living*, he says, "While my high-paying, high prestige job made me the envy of neighbors, I felt the life being sucked out of me, leaving me homesick for some place I could not name. . . . I had broken one of my own guidelines—don't get really good at something you don't want to do—and I was paying the price—an inauthentic life."[1]

It is so important that we give the world our authentic gifts and talents, but how can we do this if we don't know who we are?

WAKING UP TO OUR AUTHENTICITY

There are no role models for waking up—waking up is not something that society regularly condones or endorses. Waking up involves challenging the status quo. It's for brave hearts.

—GRACE CIROCCO, *JOURNEY TO THE SELF*

Regardless of the catalyst, "waking up" can and does shake up the soul. There are sure to be thrills and chills along the way. Waking up can be a curse or a blessing, depending on your attitude. The journey can be messy, varied, and long, but also beautiful, inspiring, and adventurous. Waking up is the soul's destiny. It is your right, not a privilege. It's all part of the plan, the unfolding of the Mystery. But how does one go about it?

Seeking to live the authentic life is an ancient quest. We have been searching for the truth forever, it seems. When we pull out the dictionary, we learn that the word "authentic" means "genuine, not false or fictitious, original." Is that what you see when you look in the mirror?

It is unlikely that people will embark on a spiritual quest for their authentic Self without some prompting or an external "wake-up call." First of all, we don't have time. We haven't learned the secret of stopping our lives in order to examine them. So for some of us, wake-up calls are inevitable. These are events such as personal tragedies, brushes with death, illnesses, the loss of a job or friendship, divorce, or betrayal. They can also come with the passing of time, when we've celebrated yet another birthday ending in zero.

After one of my seminars a man came up to me in tears to share with me his wake-up call. He was responding to research I had shared with the class that showed how men and women react differently to stress. When women have too many demands on their time, they will make sure they do a good job at work, as well as take care of their family responsibilities at home. What gets put on the back burner are exercise and girlfriends, the very things women need in order to cope with stress. For men, it's different. When men feel the pressure, they will deliver the goods at work and still manage to make time for exercise, but the one thing that gets set aside is family.[2]

"I thought that if I kept bringing the paycheck home, I was okay," he told me, wiping the tears from his eyes. "I was worried about getting fired at work. What I didn't realize was that I could get fired at home."

"What happened?" I asked. As soon as I spoke, I wanted to take my words back, because his chin began to tremble again.

"I came home one day to find that my wife and two young daughters had left. She later divorced me."

That had been a big wake-up call for him, and he obviously still needed to heal. He's not alone. So many of us don't know what's important until it's too late.

My friend Melanie, who is an aesthetician, runs her own business. She's worked extremely hard over the past two years to establish a solid clientele, so I haven't seen much of her. Recently, her aunt, to whom she had been very close, died suddenly. It was a shock to everyone, and it made Melanie feel sad, reflective, and thoughtful about her life.

"It sure has made me realize a few things," she told me, "like who's important to me and whom I want to spend time with, and how precious life is. I have been working way too hard."

Wake-up calls come in all shapes and sizes. They come

unannounced, and they can cause us immense grief. No one knows why bad things happen to us. Sometimes we want to scream, "Why me, God?" But if we face adversity square in the eye and work through the feelings—the fear, anxiety, and turmoil such experiences produce—they can act as purification for the Spirit, a way for us to grow our souls. "Each problem is an assignment designed by your soul," the author of *Why Me, Why This, Why Now?* teaches. Robin Norwood recommends the view that adversity is a path to our healing and that suffering has meaning, purpose, and dignity.[3]

Wake-up calls, although painful, bring us closer to who we are. They can begin our journey—a spiritual journey—to discovering our authentic core. The spiritual journey is the voyage back home to our Self. We're going back to our roots. We're reconnecting with our Spirit.

"This journey is not easy," my client Tom would tell me when he came for his weekly coaching session. Tom's wake-up call came at fifty-two, when he was told by his company that he was no longer needed. He had known some cuts had to be made, but never thought his position would be affected. Although he was shocked at first, today—three years later—Tom feels renewed, invigorated. He's learned some pretty amazing things along the way. For one, he's found out that the computer industry in which he was working was corroding his soul. He had been ignoring his body's signals that his health was failing. He also had been ignoring what mattered most to him: his wife and children. During his two-year journey, he also discovered that he has the heart of an artist. Today Tom paints, and he has managed to sell some of his paintings to friends and on the Internet. He says, "It makes me happy to know that I am giving the world what my authentic Self wants to give, rather than what my boss wanted me to give."

We are, in the end, like that beautiful phoenix that flames and dies, only to be reborn from the ashes into a magnificent new creation. We are all works in progress.

What wake-up calls have you had? What do you need to pay attention to? What teachers have arrived on your doorstep? What wisdom is your soul ready for? Every event in your life is a teacher, a messenger from the unconscious. The Buddha said that our only job is to wake up. Wake up your soul to this possibility, and you will look with new eyes at your life.

Taking Off Our Masks

**The soul would much rather fail in its own life
than succeed at someone else's.**

—DAVID WHYTE

How do we wake up from our sleep? How do we wake up to our magnificence, to our divinity, to the fact that we are living, breathing, walking, talking miracles? One way is to begin removing our masks.

We are conditioned by advertising and the popular media to feel skeptical about our appearances, our failures, and our personality flaws. To feel good again, we assume various masks to try to please the people around us. Sometimes we put on these masks as children in order to cope with loss, abandonment, or a dysfunctional family. Sometimes we assume the masks out of fear—fear of pain, fear that we won't be loved, fear that we'll fail, fear of abandonment. We take on the masks because we have somehow bought into the belief that our authentic Self is not okay. It requires honesty to recognize our various masks, and courage to peel them off and live authentically. To express who we are to the world, we must first become aware of who we are and who we are not.

If you can, seek solitude. The false Self tends to come out in the presence of others. The true Self is more likely to emerge when you're alone. Arrange a stretch of uninterrupted time; perhaps take a long walk alone or sit in a quiet comfortable place. I love going to the forest near my home, where I have a favorite log that I sit on. I go there to get in touch with *Grace*. When I was a child growing up on a fruit farm, I'd go to the canal behind our farm to write in my journal, "Sam." Perhaps when you were a child, you had such a place, too. What about now? Find a place where you can celebrate your solitude. Whether it's at home or out in nature, you need someplace where you can be alone.

Then turn to the following two questions (or write the questions in your journal now and think about them at the park tomorrow, or when you're driving home from work, or while you're soaking in the tub). Let these questions plant a seed in your mind and let the answers come forth when they're ready. When you have insights, though, it's important that you write them down.

- **Who do I pretend to be, and with whom?** For example, "I pretend to be strong with my kids" or "I pretend to know it all with my boss" or "I pretend to be in control with my customers."
- **What do I risk by being me?** For example, "I risk being judged harshly" or "I risk being hurt" or "I risk feeling out of control."

Then take a look at the masks listed on page 17. Many are masks that we assume unconsciously. Over time, these masks become perceived as our identities; peeling them off is difficult. This is part of the Self-discovery journey. We need to strip away this pretension to find our buried truth within.

not enough	self-sufficient
too much	super mom/dad
the perfectionist	stoic
tough guy	busy bee
know-it-all	caretaker of the world
have-it-all	victim
done-it-all	martyr
nice guy/gal	saint
class clown	flirt
weaker sex	judge
party animal	rebel
dumb blonde	expert
workaholic	

- Which of these masks do you know that you wear?
- What would you lose if you took them off?
- How does wearing these masks alienate you from your authentic Self?
- Which ones are you ready to say good-bye to?

The first step in removing these assumed masks is to be aware of them. Be conscious of when the masks come on and with whom. Who pushes your buttons? Many of us have been socialized to sacrifice our authentic Self in order to meet society's expectations. In pleasing everyone else, we have lost our unique personhood. After we have assumed layers of masks, reconnecting with the authentic core can be an arduous task.

MASKS AND RELATIONSHIPS

**At breakfast a beloved asked her lover,
"Who do you love more, yourself or me?"**
—RUMI

The authentic Self comes out when we feel safe. What are you like with your best friend? Your parents? Your childhood friends? Your neighbors? Your colleagues at work? Your boss? Your lover? Your children? My experience is that we allow different parts of ourselves to come out at different times, depending on how safe we feel in the relationship. When we feel unconditionally loved and accepted, we are relaxed enough to leave the masks behind and bring out our authentic Self.

Think about masks and your relationships, and ask yourself:

• Whom do you allow to see the real you?
• Which relationships bring out your deepest and most authentic Self?
• With whom do you feel vulnerable?
• What masks do you wear with your employer?
• What masks do you wear with your parents or siblings?
• What masks, if any, do you wear with your significant other?

There are times when both parties in a relationship put on their masks. This is perfectly normal in situations where something is at stake. Take, for example, two people negotiating the sale of a house. The seller says the house is perfect. To hasten the purchase, she wants the buyer to know that there is plenty of interest in the home. The buyer, on the other hand, wants the seller to think that he too has other options, and doesn't show much emotion, even if he loves the house. Both are protecting their own interests. Both have a hidden agenda.

But sometimes people do show their vulnerabilities, their fears, their hopes and dreams. They share both their pain and their joy. They are not afraid to be who they are because they know, regardless of the demons they take out of the closet, that they will not be judged or rejected. These relationships are the most sacred to us and make our lives worth living. We can take risks in such relationships, with the knowledge that, should conflict arise, it's okay. We have faith that all will be well and that love and acceptance will always be at the core. The people with whom I can share all of me and risk being truly authentic, I call my soulmates. Soulmates are connected on a spiritual level. They've shared past lives together. There is deep understanding and comfort between them. Conflict becomes but a spoonful of water in the vast ocean of Love.

MASKS AND EMOTIONS

When you share your joy with me,
you tell me what you belong to.
—ORIAH MOUNTAIN DREAMER

Sometimes we bring our authentic, vulnerable Self out into the world like an enthusiastic puppy—only to run up against the masks of others. When this happens, we feel not only foolish, but also deeply betrayed. I had such an experience about ten years ago. I was part of a women's healing group that met once a week. We were preparing to go on a weekend retreat, and our leader wanted to take us through an exercise that would gauge how safe and comfortable we felt with each other. We were going to be doing some intensive "inner work" on the weekend, so it was important that we felt safe enough to bring out our authentic selves.

Our facilitator gave each of us a sheet of paper with the names of all the women in the group, and three sets of stickers. Red stickers were like red lights. They meant, "Stop! I'm not comfortable with you. I have an issue with you." (Basically they meant, "I don't like you.") Yellow stickers were like amber lights: Proceed, but only with caution. Getting a yellow sticker meant, "I don't really know you. I could feel comfortable, but I need to talk to you more." Green stickers were green lights. The message was, "I like you. I feel comfortable with you." After we had placed stickers beside all the names, we were told to meet each person individually to share how we felt about them.

Being who I am, I gave most people a green light. There were only a few ambers, but that was because I had missed a few sessions and hadn't gotten to know everyone in the group yet. Then, after I told one woman—I'll call her "Sue"—all the reasons why I had given her a green light, she responded with all the reasons why she had given me a red one. I remember the horrendous confusion and hurt that swelled inside me. I was shocked, especially because I had been totally loving and generous in my praise of her.

She had a problem, she said, with the way I blurted things out in the group, the way I was always asking everybody questions. She also had a problem with my "bubbly personality" and my "sickening enthusiasm." In short, I was too intense, too loud, and too much for her, and she didn't think she could feel comfortable around me. I couldn't believe my ears. If she felt this way about me, why hadn't I picked up on it sooner? How could I have been so naïve? Her words wounded me to the core. I spent the rest of the evening alone, too ashamed to face the others. It took a lot of courage and prompting from the leader and the rest of the group before she and I even considered going on the weekend, but eventually we both decided to go.

That weekend, during a psychodrama re-enactment of a dream, I learned things about Sue that opened my eyes and my heart to her. What came out was that, as a little girl, Sue had been much like me—passionate, excitable, always bubbly, asking everyone lots of questions. Her mother didn't like her that way, and one day in a fit of anger, she poured boiling water over Sue's arms to shut her up. From that day forward, Sue took on the mask of "reserved, quiet little girl" and buried the part of herself that her mother did not accept and love. The adult Sue had been unaware that her authentic Self was more like me. Instead, she hated anybody who reminded her of the person she wasn't allowed to be. That weekend experience was not only an eye-opener, but a soul-opener, too. It brought healing and forgiveness to our relationship and to the group as a whole. I became Sue's unofficial coach, encouraging her to put her "quiet" mask aside and let her authentic Self come out to play with me.

We put on our masks to protect ourselves, and while we were children, they worked. But now it's time to ask yourself some questions. Do your masks represent who you truly are? Are they betraying you? What are your emotional triggers? Could the "difficult" people in your life be aspects of your buried Self? Could these people provide the keys to unlock some of your unconscious masks? Are you projecting your masks onto the people in your life?

Masks keep us from uniting with our authentic Self. They prevent us from experiencing the joy, love, and freedom that are our birthright. They also prevent us from crossing the bridge towards our dreams and the life we want. Wake up. Think. Be aware of anyone who causes you to put on a mask, and think about why you do so. The *why* may be a sign that it's time for you to set your masks aside and bring forth your authentic core, your authentic Voice. Go deep. Connect with your inner child. Do some soul work. Mourn for the person you were not allowed to be. Expose the unconscious masks and let go of them. Better yet, have a ceremony—bury them and say good-bye.

THE LAST OF THE MASKS

We are not meant to stay wounded. By staying stuck in the power of our wounds, we block our own transformation.
—CAROLINE MYSS

Don't be fooled by the tricky masks. Those are the ones that appear to give us feelings of self-worth, even an identity. They are the ones to come off last. Take, for example, Elaine, a dear neighbor of mine. She was always in pain. She had sustained a back injury in a car accident several years ago. Despite what her doctor and friends recommended—craniosacral massage, acupuncture, chiropractic, hydrotherapy—Elaine didn't seek any help. I couldn't understand this, until one day when I saw her with a group of people. It was summertime, and the neighbors were gardening or walking their dogs. I watched as she told people about her back-pain woes, skillfully evoking sympathy from each. "Poor Elaine," everyone would say. "How do you get through the day?"

I realized then that Elaine was married to her pain, and that as long as she got that reaction from people, she was going to wear that mask of pain. She was getting the attention and sympathy she craved, but she was also stuck in her illness. A few months later, I read about this exact phenomenon (called *woundology*) in Caroline Myss's book *Why People Don't Heal and How They Can*. Here's what Myss says:

> I began to discern when a person was genuinely going through the specific stage of healing that requires a witness and when someone had discovered the "street" value or social currency of their wound—that is, the manipulative value of the wound.[4]

I will discuss wounds and healing in more detail in chapter 4 (Heal Your Past), but for now, ask yourself whether any of your masks are protecting your self-esteem. What would you lose if you took them off?

THE QUEST FOR AUTHENTICITY

**Seek not abroad; turn back into thyself,
for in the inner man dwells the truth.**
—ST. AUGUSTINE

My husband and I had been reading Anthony de Mello's book *Awareness*. One day, while visiting our Mexican friends, we found the same book on their shelves, except that it was a Spanish translation. I found it interesting that the title of the Spanish version was *Despierta!*, which means not exactly "awareness," but more like "wake up!" I began to think about the relationship between these two concepts. We need to be aware in order to wake up, but we need to wake up in order to be aware! So be aware of events that come disguised as problems in your life—your wake-up calls. And then be observant (or aware) of the people, places, and events that you call into your life.

Let me take you back to a time when I was a student at Queen's University in Kingston, Ontario. Many universities and colleges sponsor writers-in-residence, who are invited to live on campus and interact with students. In my first year of university, I got to meet and become quite close to one such writer.

Most days after class, we'd go strolling—often arm in arm, Italian-style—across the campus. It was autumn; I have beautiful memories of crunching through leaves beside the pale limestone buildings. This gentle man of letters shared with me his philosophy on life. "Be always observant, Graziella," he'd say in his native Italian. "A good writer observes even the tiniest of details. One must observe, or else life goes by, and you miss it."

Then we'd stand still and observe the wind on our faces, or the squirrels in the trees, or the crashing waves of Lake Ontario. Sometimes students would walk past and he would whisper, "What did you observe in that relationship? What did you see on her face? His face?" He told me that his job as a writer was to observe the world and then to report back his findings.

What if someone were commissioned to write a book about your life—your thoughts, your feelings, your friends, your choices, all that you are—with nothing to go on but what you had to say? The author would be totally dependent on you for all the material. Each day you would have to report a new observation about your life. Do you think you would start to pay more attention to your world? Do you think you might wake up to your life, to the magnificence that is you? Do you think you would become more aware of your feelings and of the conversations you have inside your head?

Recently I heard David Whyte speak at a conference. He's the author of *Poetry and the Preservation of Soul in Corporate America*, as well as several collections of poetry. He kept stressing to the audience the importance of "conversation." At work, if we don't maintain conversations with colleagues and customers, we lose them. At home, not maintaining a conversation with our mate and children means we lose those relationships. And if we don't maintain the internal conversation with ourselves, we end up losing the Self. The quest for authenticity begins when we start to pay attention to that conversation.

PAY ATTENTION TO YOUR FEELINGS

**For too long we have been blind to the
cognitive riches of feeling!**

—JOHN O'DONAHUE

A powerful way to get to know who you are is through your feelings. Feelings are sacred. They don't lie. They are a vehicle for the expression of your authentic Self. They will say who you are perhaps more than anything else. That's why we need to pay attention to them. We learn when we are young that to survive in the "real world" we must fake it, put aside our feelings, get rid of our vulnerabilities, and not show people how much we are hurting. We have learned to hide our authentic feelings, especially if they are negative.

Anger is one of the most threatening of emotions, and children learn from a young age that it is unacceptable to express it. Rather than retaliate or abandon children when they get angry, parents need to let them have access to all their feelings. Parents must survive the anger and the hatred and find a way to return unconditional love. The relationship between parent and child is bound to involve upsets and conflict. This is a normal part of any relationship. However, if parents are emotionally needy, insecure, or depressed, they can't offer unconditional acceptance when their children display unhappy emotions. As a result, some of us learned as children to shut down our anger and turn off our passion and intensity. Without knowing it, we put our parents' needs ahead of our own, creating false impressions of who we were just to get the love and approval we craved.

The consequence is that we have both surface feelings and deep ones. If you're angry, what are you afraid of? If you're hurting, what makes you sad? Gently quiet any thoughts and focus on feelings. Some people are so out of tune with their feelings that when you ask them how they feel, they'll give you a judgment, a statement, or a thought. Your feelings are waiting to give you so much wisdom, if only you would listen. More than anything else, they bubble up from your authentic core, and can be the impetus for embarking on your spiritual journey. A lot of current literature describes the benefits of becoming more "heart-centered"; I will discuss this concept in more detail in chapter 4.

PAY ATTENTION TO YOUR DREAMS

Dreams begin to awaken us to the fact that we are spiritual or interdimensional beings . . . they are like a letter from the higher self to the conscious mind.
—BETTY BETHARDS

Dreams have been known to predict the future, save lives, solve mysteries, and unlock the key to our authentic Self. They are the highway to the unconscious. Sleep research centers have found that we need to sleep because we need to dream. We need to visit the unconscious world—the world of dreams—and we need to do so on a daily basis.

I've always been fascinated by the dream state. Where exactly do we go when we dream? I used to love watching my babies sleeping because I could see them dreaming. Their eyes would move from side to side, and their faces would break into bright smiles. My grandmother used to tell me that babies are very connected to the spirit world and that during their dreams they are able to communicate with God and the angels.

Many therapists work with dreams to loosen emotional blockages and speed the healing process. We need to pay attention to our dreams, because they can link us with what is truly authentic in ourselves. Sometimes a dream will come to us over and over again, because we may be ignoring its message. This book started with a dream that I had many years ago, and the dream gave me its title.

Everyone dreams, but not everyone remembers their dreams. One way you can begin to remember your dreams is by making a conscious decision to do so. Before you go to bed tonight, say to yourself, "I want to remember one dream. I will remember one dream." Repeat this three times, out loud if possible. Do this several nights in a row. Keep at it; don't give up too quickly.

You also can try keeping a glass of water near your bed. Just before going to bed, drink half the glass. Tell yourself out loud, "Tomorrow when I wake up, I will drink the other half and remember one dream." In the morning, as soon as you're awake and while still in bed, drink the other half and see what happens. Some of my clients say they haven't even begun to drink the water before they're aware of something.

Another technique for remembering dreams is to wake up softly. Alarm clocks that buzz you from unconsciousness scare dreams away. If you can, wake up on your own. If you can't, then do it with soft music. Some people are awakened by their pets and others by their children—all preferable to loud mechanical noises. Then linger in bed for a minute or two, stretching your limbs and gently reaching for images from your dream world. This technique always works for me.

Make it easy to remember your dreams. Keep a journal or notepad at your bedside. When you wake up, write down what you remember before you get out of bed. Hang on to whatever images or phrases are in your mind. The act of writing them down will stimulate more dream memories. Later in the day, return to the journal. Is there anything else you remember? Write down any associations.

Pay attention to your dreams. They are whispers from the other side. If you have not paid attention to them for a long time, they may be in hiding. They need coaxing to come to the surface. Ask yourself what they are telling you. According to Carl Jung, dreams are not to be taken literally; they are symbolic interpretations of the Self. So, for example, if you dream that your mother is seriously ill, think about what your mother means to you. It may be a part of yourself, perhaps your nurturing Self, that is sick.

All dream interpretation guides are just that—guides. There can be no universal dream interpretation bible because everyone is different. In the end, you are the best judge of what your dreams may be trying to tell you. Ask yourself whether the dream situations or emotions remind you of anything that is going on in your waking life. What associations do you make with the people and events in your dreams? What themes can you see emerging over time? Making a mental note to remember your dreams, discussing them with those closest to you or with a professional, writing them down—all these things will tell your subconscious mind that you respect its wisdom. The more it is respected, the more information it will give you as to who you really are. Dreams are a vehicle to help you expose the unconscious masks you have assumed over the years. Pay attention to them.

PAY ATTENTION TO YOUR WORLD

Nobody sees a flower—really—it is so small it takes time— we haven't time—and to see takes time . . .

—GEORGIA O'KEEFFE

My husband is short-sighted. He was eleven years old the day he got his first pair of glasses. He recalls the excitement he felt that first day looking through the lenses that would reveal what the world was really like. "It was amazing," he told me. "Everything was so crystal-clear. I could actually look at a tree and see the individual leaves on it. Leaves! Up until then, I didn't know leaves were something you could see except from very close up." He told me he spent hours that first week walking around his neighborhood observing everything that he had missed without glasses. "It was as if I was seeing everything for the first time."

What if you tried on a pair of glasses that allowed you to look at your life with more clarity? What would you see? What if you could look at life with awe and childlike wonder? How different might your life be? What if your magic glasses helped you see everyone with more compassion, more love? Would your life change at all? Look around you. Open the eyes of your soul. What do you see? Be observant of everything, and you will discover things that will help you find your way—your unique place in the Universe.

Angeles Arrien, the American anthropologist and author of the *The Four-Fold Way*, shares her wisdom with her four rules for living. It's interesting that rule number two is "Pay attention." That means "be aware, be observant, be conscious." Different words—one message.

TASHI DELEY

**The problem of the meaning of life is solved
by the mystery of love.**
—SAM KEEN

Sometimes we discover who we truly are through the eyes of another. When we feel loved to the core, we feel understood, blessed, liberated. I've discovered that one of the reasons why couples fall out of love is that they no longer feel "seen" by their partners. I don't mean seen with the physical eyes, but on a different, more spiritual level. When you see your beloved with the eyes of your heart and of your soul, you can penetrate to their very Essence, to that abundant Light that the Creator put in all of us.

I asked a good friend and longtime confidante when it was that she fell out of love with her ex-husband. She told me it happened while she was expecting her third child. Even though it was the third time around, she felt excited to be once more carrying God's miracle within her. But her husband wasn't awake to that miracle. "He barely noticed me," she recalled. "He made it seem like it was routine, not special at all." She felt so alone and sad throughout that pregnancy. Even though the decision to have a third child had been mutual, he could not allow himself to see it fresh as if for the first time. He could not see his wife's beauty and radiance. He could not see the Spirit of their unborn child.

When we're not seen for whom we are, we disconnect. We mourn. The Tibetan people have a traditional greeting. When they see each other, they put their hands together palm to palm, fingers pointing up, in front of their chest, bow and say the words *"Tashi deley."* The words mean, "I honor the magnificence in you." Isn't that beautiful? Imagine what a kinder, gentler world it would be if everyone greeted each other in such a holy way. Imagine saying hello to your boss, colleague, or neighbor that way. Imagine saluting the magnificence in your friends. Imagine giving recognition to the Light in your children every day. *Tashi deley* expresses a deep reverence for one another. It is what our world needs today. It would help us realize who we are if the people around us would, at least on occasion, reflect our magnificence.

The Tibetans are a gentle people. I had an opportunity to meet some of them in a refugee camp in Darjeeling, India. Even though the political oppression in their country means they must live as transients, displaced from their families, they can still use their spiritual eyes to bless one another. When they thanked me for buying some of their handiwork—crafts and sweaters they sell in order to stay self-sufficient—their eyes were warm and moist. They *saw* me in a way that was far different from any other exchanges I've had. I left them feeling blessed. It's perhaps fitting that their spiritual leader, the Dalai Lama, says that his religion is compassion. The Tibetans know how to communicate compassion and kindness with their eyes. They see straight into your God Essence.

In the past, it used to bother me when I noticed parents acting indifferent towards their children. I'm sure they loved them, but rarely did I see a parent who knew how to soak up their children with their eyes, who could *see* the miracles their children were. How sad this made me. I was puzzled as to why these parents behaved so casually around their precious offspring. I vowed to myself that I would never take my own kids for granted, never allow their presence to become commonplace, to be anything less than holy.

My children are twelve and ten as I write this, and I'm sure I've broken that promise many times. No one is immune to bad days or stress. The clock ticks on, and there are days when we forget our own magnificence, let alone see it in others. I encourage you to see your children as much as possible with new eyes. Celebrate the perfect souls that they are. Recognize the Divine spark in each of them. Witness the miracle of their birth every time you lay eyes on them.

Next time you see your beloved, drink him in. Spend a few minutes staring into his or her eyes. What does the poet say? The eyes are the windows of the soul. What stories does the soul hide? What treasures lie buried and undiscovered? Who is this person? Before you make love, *see* your beloved! See the beauty and the abundance; salute the magnificence. Say hello to the God within.

LIVE YOUR TRUTH

The truth is always simple, but living it is not always easy.
—REV. ALFRED MILLER

Often the reason that people can't take action is uncertainty. They've lost the connection to their internal compass; their truth. Before we take the step, we must be authentic. We must clarify what we want and where we want to go. And then we must *live* our truth.

One of my clients, a married woman, came to me one day because she was consumed with love for another man. "Mary" (which is not her real name) was in her mid-thirties, with two children and a decent, loving husband. She explained to me that she hadn't been looking for another relationship, but this love had taken her heart totally by surprise and wouldn't let go. The affair had been going on for about six months, but now she had decided to pull the plug. However, she was absolutely sickened by the thought of never seeing her lover again. I advised Mary to write a letter to him. Whether she gave it to him or not, at least it would help her clarify her thoughts on seeing him again. The following week, she brought me the letter.

Dear Love of My Life:

I don't know why your angel eyes entered me so deeply last April. I was relatively happy in my own little world last spring when I first felt the burn of your penetrating gaze. Why me? I thought. Why is he looking at me? I remember how strange and awkward it was to tell you my name; me, a happily married woman. I knew then that that was the beginning of the end, that we were destined to be. We were drawn to each other from the very beginning, like some sort of weird cosmic destiny.

I know that we are both married, but essentially we belong to no one except perhaps to that Infinite Universe from which we came. We are who we are—and we're all here on borrowed time. Our stories unfolded so naturally, softly, gently, like leaves falling one by one in the autumn air. It feels like I've known you my whole life. It was destiny that brought us together so we could reconnect from the past and weave our present moments together.

People come and people go in our lives and our hearts know who to trust and who to love. And sometimes our hearts feel things that the so-called "rule-book" says are wrong. Why is our loving each other wrong? Because we're married, because it's considered "betrayal." But I love both of you! You and my

33

husband, just in different ways. Why is this so difficult for people to understand? Why is it that I can love more than one female friend, more than one child, and yet only one man? I've always admired the loons who mate for life, and yet, even though I know I've mated for life with my husband, I can't imagine a world where I can't love you, too. I heard that even though the loons mate for life, they always winter apart. Perhaps if couples adopted this practice, they might be able to keep passion alive.

You said to me once, "We're on a train that's going nowhere." I think it's time we got off the train. I don't want to lie anymore. Our families need us. We can't abandon them, and I can't keep seeing you behind his back. The guilt is eating at me. I'm a mess. I can't cope with it any longer.

I want you to know that you've brought infinite joy to my life, and for that, I am eternally grateful. I feel I've been blessed. And I wasn't looking for this. You found the key to my heart and slipped in before I had the chance to realize what was happening.

I'll always keep your memory locked inside me like a tender secret, your beautiful eyes imprinted on my soul, your smile etched in my mind, your words printed on my heart. My life is, and will always be, richer because you were in it. Look for me in your next life. I will be there waiting for you. My love for you is eternal.

Mary could barely read it to me, she was crying so much. But it was important for her to read her words aloud to see if they still rang true.

"Are you sure this is what you want to do?" I asked her. "Are you sure this is your truth?"

"No, it is society's truth, not mine," she exclaimed angrily through her tears.

"What do you mean?"

"The moral ethics of the day don't approve of what I am doing."

"Do you approve of what you're doing?"

"Yes . . . no . . . I mean, why did God send this to me if it were such a bad thing?"

"Good question. Why did God send it to you?" I asked.

"To help me fall in love with myself and life again. To bring joy to my life. To make me realize that life is precious and I should not take one single minute of it for granted." Then she began to cry again. "Why, Grace? Why can't I love both of them? Why do I have to make a choice?"

"Why do you feel you must make a choice?"

"Because I'm not supposed to have my cake and eat it, too, I guess. I don't know."

"Well, what stops you from living your truth?" I asked.

"My guilt. I feel like I'm betraying my husband," Mary said.

"Are you?"

"Technically, according to the Ten Commandments, yes. But not really. In my heart I feel like I'm a better wife, a better mother, a better version of myself. But if my husband found out, he would never forgive me. He would be devastated. We'd probably break up."

SELF-BETRAYAL

This above all: to thine own self be true.

—HAMLET

There will be times in your life when you reach a fork in the road. Choose one path, and you betray yourself. Choose the other path, and you betray someone else. Either way, there will

35

be suffering. Too many people avoid embracing their truth because they want to avoid pain. When faced with such life choices, they will take the path of least resistance, in the naïve belief that self-betrayal is the path of least pain!

If Mary betrays her husband, she will live with constant guilt and anxiety that he might find out. If he finds out, the marriage might end. Those are the consequences. But if she betrays herself, what then are the consequences? What happens to people when they betray their souls? There will be pain, unbearable pain. Will this lead to resentment? Bitterness? Illness? I've had clients in similar situations who ended up resenting their spouses, and the resentment led to fault-finding, arguments, and eventually separation. So what they were trying to prevent from happening happened anyway.

Too often we're trained to keep our promises and our agreements with others, but not those we make with ourselves. But what about our souls? The soul knows. How can we grow self-respect if we're betraying our own truth? How can we have integrity if we betray what is right for us? And yet we do it every day. We make a big deal when others betray us, but don't blink an eyelash when we do it to ourselves.

Those of us who approach life as martyrs—the ones who say, "What I want doesn't matter. It's what you want that is most important"—are usually liked and even celebrated compared to those empowered brave hearts who are true to themselves. If we sacrifice our truth for the sake of another, if we swallow our feelings and "do the right thing," then we're considered heroes. Since marriage is a pretty big commitment, considerable guilt and shame are associated with a breakup, regardless of how difficult the marriage has become. When my aunt left my uncle almost thirty years ago, she was completely shunned by her community. Even my mother, who is the most compassionate person I know, judged her harshly for leaving her family. Oriah Mountain Dreamer, in *The Invitation*, wonders, "I want to know if you can disappoint another and be true to yourself; if you can bear the accusation of betrayal and not betray your own soul; . . .⁵" Being true to oneself today is not easy, but we must face this challenge if we are to lead authentic lives.

I tried to encourage Mary to listen to her truth, to explore other possibilities, perhaps even discuss her infidelity with her husband. But she was adamant her husband would never understand. Besides, she said, she believed her destiny was the same as the heroine's in *The Bridges of Madison County*. Francesca didn't go off with her lover because she wouldn't turn her back on "a good man" and her two children. She would sooner sacrifice her happiness than destroy the happiness of her family.

Almost six months later, Mary started experiencing severe abdominal pain. She was devastated when she found out she had a malignant tumor in her uterus. After her surgery, she spent considerable time wondering why this had happened to her. When we talked about it, she told me she had figured out what the tumor was about.

"It's a punishment," she said. "Not because I committed adultery, but because I said good-bye to him before my heart was ready. Grace, I betrayed my heart."

After she broke off the affair, Mary had gone through considerable agony. She was an emotional mess, grieving the love she had lost. Because her husband didn't know anything about it, she had to pretend that everything was okay. She told me that some days the pain got so bad, all she wanted was to crawl into a hole and die.

We're holistic creatures. When we betray our truth, we can call illness into our lives. Psychoneuroimmunologists like Herbert

Benson, Joan Borysenko, and Hans Selye, all pioneers in the mind-body connection, have found a link between disease and what we think and feel. Norman Shealy, founder of the American Holistic Medical Association and co-author of *The Creation of Health*, wrote that 75 percent of his patients told him they wanted to die six to twenty-four months before they were diagnosed with cancer. When I shared this information with Mary, she was shocked.

"Do you think I'm going to die?" she asked me.

"I don't know, Mary. Do you want to die?"

"I don't want to anymore. But last year, when the pain was so bad, I wanted to disappear."

It's been a long road for Mary, but she is now determined to live life to the fullest. She eventually told her husband the truth, and together they began to heal their marriage. She doesn't regret what happened and has decided that she will never betray her heart again.

When we betray ourselves, it may seem like the right thing in the short term, but in the long term, nobody wins. In the past few years, many of my clients and friends have been at similar crossroads in their lives. I don't know why the miracle of Love comes to us when it does. But every day, in cities and towns all around the world, married people are falling in love. And then they must decide: "Do I betray myself or my promise to them? Do I break my heart or theirs?" I think it's one of the toughest choices we'll ever have to make. It's choices like these—especially if you don't shrink back, especially if you can live through them and embrace the highs and lows regardless of the outcome—that grow your soul.

LOVE AND TRUTH

Where do love, and truth abide;
Like birds of a feather, side by side.
Only to find, that in the end
They are as one, an only friend.
And where are we, adrift in a mire
Consoled by life, and a longing desire
To rid our sins, of days, in the past
And hallo the future, with the truth at last.
—NICHOLAS OLENICK

It happens to many of us. We have children and we soon get caught up in the banalities of everyday life—those "practical details of living." We don't make the time to look our beloved in the eye and remind ourselves why we fell in love with him or her. Passion dries up. We no longer see the beauty in ourselves. Life loses its shine.

According to the statistics, extra-marital affairs bring a couple closer only 40 percent of the time. If there's truth and understanding between the couple, a love affair can be an opportunity to address what needs healing in the marriage, to kick-start more passion and commitment, to create intimacy. But this transparency requires courage, and most people fear confrontation. Please don't shrink back from those experiences your soul calls into your life, regardless of how messy they are. *Life* is messy. Please don't sacrifice your truth to avoid the mess.

For many people, the pressure to sacrifice their truth—to betray themselves—is too strong. The inner tyrant—that voice inside their heads put there by years of social conditioning, says they must follow tradition, religion, or the "rules" of the day. When will we turn within for our answers?

How about you? When was the last time you betrayed yourself? Was it years ago or just recently? To be aware of self-betrayal, you must stay awake to your feelings. Some of us betray ourselves in tiny, meaningless ways every day. For others, self-betrayal has become a habit, even a chronic problem. Commit an outrageous act today. Do what *you* want for a change! Go with *your* feelings—stop denying yourself joy! Ask yourself when and with whom do you swallow your truth. Why do you hide your authentic Self? How often do you accommodate others? Why do you give in?

One of my clients, a man in his forties, took a job just to pay the bills. He had been downsized by his company, so when a friend suggested him to his boss and put in a good word for him, he felt he couldn't refuse. To show loyalty and appreciation to his friend, he betrayed himself. He completely lost his enthusiasm for life and had to go on antidepressants. His relationship with his friend soured when he lost the company a huge contract. He had realized it was not his type of work, but had ignored what his heart was telling him.

What symptoms have you experienced because you did not follow your own inner guidance?

We tend to discard our personal stories—what is true for us—for the truth of another. Why do we do this? Why do we sell out? We carry with us the truth of our ancestors, the truth of our convictions, the truth inside our hearts. Yet every day we close our ears to it so that we can hear other words, worlds away.

I know that for some of us the voice of fear speaks loudly. It prevents us from taking the step to cross the bridge. It is the reason why we betray ourselves. How can we overcome the fear? Ask yourself, "What am I afraid of? What will I lose?" Don't let fear run your life! You must be willing to face your fears squarely if you want to take a stab at living authentically—living the life your soul came here to live. Regardless of how others may judge you, in the end this is your life. If not now, when?

The poet David Whyte reminds us that the soul would rather fail at its own life than succeed at someone else's. Remember, nothing holy has ever been achieved through denial. Maybe you are willing to walk through the fire and see where your soul wants to take you. Do you need to wash away your shame? Come out of the closet. There is no shame in being true to yourself; there is no shame in telling yourself the truth. There will be a time, if you haven't already experienced it, when you find yourself at the crossroads. Turn left, and you betray someone; turn right, and you betray yourself. Tell me, which will you choose?

TELL THE TRUTH

**The greatest of all true things is a true heart. Without truth
no happiness, though you try a million tricks.**

—KABIR

I know that truth for many people is an incredible risk. Many people don't tell the truth because they fear the consequences. Sometimes I think we don't give people enough credit. We just assume they can't handle the truth.

But telling the truth is also difficult because it requires that we have faith—faith in ourselves, faith in the other person, and faith in the strength of the relationship. Relationships deepen when we communicate our feelings. Have you ever taken a risk with someone by telling them how you really feel, only to find out later that they crossed you off their friendship list? Sometimes truth backfires. It depends on how you do it— whether you come from a place of revenge and hostility or from a place of love and understanding.

In most cases, however, and if the relationship is worth keeping, truth told with compassion can deepen the bond. Truth allows us to climb to higher peaks of intimacy with each other. Truth helps us to heal old wounds. Without truth, there is no trust, and without trust, there is no foundation for a relationship.

A friend I'll call "Joe" works as an undercover cop in the drug squad of a large North American city. One of the reasons his job is so stressful, he says, is because he has to tell lies all day long. To gain a drug dealer's trust, he must lie about who he is and what he wants. At the end of each day, he makes meticulous notes of all the lies he's told and to whom. He studies them and continues the pretense each following day until he has enough information to make a bust. Joe's in his forties, but he looks ten years older. His job is stressful, but I think it's the burden of lying all day long that has aged him.

In 1945, in a cave at Nag Hammadi in Upper Egypt, a hidden library of early Christian writings was found. Included in those writings was the Gospel of Thomas. An interesting part of this writing tells of the disciples asking "the living Jesus" for direction on practical matters. Jesus gives no specifics, saying only, "Do not tell lies, and do not do what you hate: for all things are manifest in the sight of heaven."[6]

Do not tell lies and do not do what you hate. That is the only advice Jesus had for his disciples. In other words, tell the truth (to others) and be true to yourself (that is, do not do what you hate). It all comes down to this: Have the courage to tell the truth and then live it. Knowing who your authentic Self is and then acting on it are what taking the step is all about.

PRACTICE INTEGRITY: WALK YOUR TALK

Today, millions are experiencing the pangs of hunger in passive helplessness. How can I speak to these millions or identify myself with them, without undertaking this fast and knowing myself what pangs of hunger mean?

—MAHATMA GANDHI

A woman who wanted her son to stop eating sugar visited the great Mahatma Gandhi in his village. "Come back in two weeks," the great master told her.

When she returned, Gandhi said to the boy, "Son, don't eat sugar. It's bad for you."

The woman looked puzzled and asked him, "Why couldn't you give my son that message two weeks ago?"

Gandhi smiled. "Two weeks ago, madam, *I* was eating sugar."

Integrity is not saying one thing and doing another. Integrity requires that your outer actions match your inner values. Imagine two pillars. One pillar represents everything that is sacred to you, everything that you value—your ethics and your principles. The second pillar represents how you think, behave, and act every day. If both pillars match—if they are the same height and width—then your life reflects integrity. If the pillars don't match, there is a lack of integrity.

The more integrity you have, the more self-respect you gain. The greater your self-respect, the more you can nurture action. You'll have integrity when you keep your promises—including those you make to yourself. You'll have integrity when you live not according to someone else's desires, but according to your own version of what is true. You'll have integrity when your principles are shaped by your inner knowing, not by your

43

external circumstances. You'll have integrity when you can stay true to your principles and values even when it seems easier to compromise your ethics and give in. You tell yourself that no one will ever know. But your silent partner knows and hears all. That silent partner is your soul.

Without integrity, we cannot feel good about ourselves. Integrity allows us to approve of ourselves. And that approval is the foundation upon which self-love and self-acceptance are based. Every day there are opportunities, circumstances, and situations where we must choose to either sacrifice our integrity or stay true to the inner compass that tells us what is right for us. Our society makes it easy for us to betray ourselves and lose integrity. You stick to the diet when people are around, but when you're alone—who will ever know? You don't yell at the kids in the grocery store, but as soon as you get in the car—you let them have it.

You may ask yourself, "Don't I have the right to do this?" Yes, but is it the right thing to do? How do you feel later on? Acting with integrity is easy when people are watching. When you are by yourself, with no audience, acting with integrity becomes more difficult. We wouldn't admit to cheating on our taxes or stealing from our company, and yet we have to live with this knowledge every second. We may think it doesn't affect us. Consciously we put it out of our mind, but our subconscious mind knows. Our Spirit—the part of us that is closest to God—knows. When we lose our integrity, we corrode our souls.

If you pay lip service to principles and ethics but don't practise them, then you are not walking your talk. If you don't walk your talk, you don't have integrity. Two of my good friends smoke. Their daughter smokes. They would like her to stop; they're worried about her health. "But how can we tell her to stop when we're not prepared to stop ourselves?" they ask me. They may be weak, but they are wise. They are not hypocrites. I think we all admire people who practice what they preach, and those who don't preach what they themselves are not willing to practice.

I believe that more of us would like to stay true to our principles—if only we knew what those principles were. That's why self-knowledge is vital. It's foundational. You must know who your authentic Self is and what is important to you before you can practice integrity. You must be willing to peel off the masks. People who walk their talk, whose character is solid, have always been admired in our society. They are the ones who can walk with their heads held high. We believe in them. We admire them. At times we even put them on a pedestal.

Another way to build integrity is to speak up when you know it's the right thing to do. We don't for a variety of reasons, and fear is the largest of those. Every day around the world, people keep their mouths shut when they know in their hearts they should be speaking up and speaking out. When was the last time you lost self-respect because you didn't speak up?

We have to acknowledge the voice within and pay respect to our inner guidance. When we refuse to put on masks for others, when we speak up and tell our truth, when we listen to our hearts, when our actions match our values, then we show our integrity. The two pillars match. Integrity nurtures self-respect. The more self-respect we have, the more action we take in our lives.

Reflections & Helpful Exercises:

1. List What Is Sacred to You

When was the last time you betrayed your truth? What, if anything, is eating away at you lately? What conversations have you had that left you uneasy and unsettled? Pay attention to those feelings. You may have compromised your ethics, and those feelings are the residue.

In your journal, divide the page in half. On one side, write down all that is sacred to you, what you believe in, what is important to you, your principles and your moral laws. On the other side of the page, write down a corresponding action step or behavior from your life that has supported that value. As you do this, you'll begin to clarify what integrity looks like to you and, perhaps, diagnose those times when you haven't been completely true to yourself.

When in doubt, ask yourself, "Do I approve of this? Do I feel good about myself? Do I respect myself? What would my soul say if it could talk to me directly? What would the person I admire most in the world say? What would God say?"

2. "Peel the Onion"

Have a partner ask you the following questions over and over again while you try to go deeper and deeper into reflection. Make sure your partner pauses after asking the question and then asks it again. Each repetition will be an invitation to dig deeper into your authentic Self. It takes time to reflect and go deep, so give yourself time. For example, your answer to "Who are you?" might be a woman, father, manager, aunt, wife, lover, piano teacher, student, etc. That is the top layer of the onion.

But when you go deeper you may find that different qualities begin to emerge. Who are you? "Sad." Who are you? "Lonely." Who

are you? "Passionate about life." Who are you? "Frightened for my
health." Who are you? "Someone who longs for intimacy."

You also can do this exercise alone in your journal. Close your
eyes and ask yourself the same question over and over again.
Then open your eyes and write down the first thing that comes to
mind. Here are some useful questions for "peeling the onion":

- Who are you?
- What do you want?
- Who do you pretend to be?
- What makes you angry?
- What makes you sad?
- What are you afraid of?
- What are you ashamed of?

*(By the way, shame is the most corrosive emotion in the human lan-
guage. Unearth your shame, face it, and really feel it, and you've done
a lot to get rid of it. More about healing emotions in chapter 4.)*

3. What Masks Do You Wear?

Write down, draw, or find symbols to represent some of the masks
you know you wear. Think about why you wear them. Then ask yourself, "What will I lose if I let them go? How do they protect me?
How do they rob me of my authenticity?" Finally, ask yourself,
"Which one am I prepared to let go?" Then have a funeral and bury
it. Dig a hole in your backyard and say good-bye. It may take you
several weeks or months to let go of one mask, and some masks
you may not be ready to let go of at all. Just do what you can and
honor where you are right now.

2

Discover Your Destiny

WHAT'S YOUR DESTINY?

There is a wick within you that is waiting to become the light of your soul. When this inner flame burns brightly, you will feel a magnificent awakening of your life.

—BRADFORD KEENEY

A few years ago, the members of Willow Creek Community Church, located near Chicago, conducted a survey in the United States. They wanted to know this: If people could ask God only one question to which they were guaranteed an answer, what would that question be? Topping the list was "Why is there suffering?" Many of us seek the answer to that question.

Three questions tied for second place, and all of them concerned destiny. They were:

1 What is the purpose or meaning of life?
2 What is going to happen in my future?

3 What is going to happen when I die?

Those who asked question 1 want to know "What is my destiny in life?" Those who asked question 2 are seeking the answer to "What is my destiny in this world?" Those who asked question 3 are asking "What is my destiny in eternity?" People today are on a spiritual quest. They long for clarity about who they are and where they're going. They want to know their destiny and the purpose of this life.

So, what is destiny? It's the root word of "destination," and comes from the Latin *destinatus* (fixed or decided). It is a question of direction: Where am I to take my life? What am I meant to do with my life? The word also conveys a sense of fate or purpose. Some people connect their fate to God's plan for them.

Your destiny contains your "mission" and the vision you hold of your life. If you understand your destiny, you will know what is waiting for you on the other side of the bridge—it motivates you to take action. I'm convinced that people don't take the step because they're not connected to their destiny. They don't see the big picture. They feel powerless, not special. Everyone's life has purpose and meaning. It's up to each of us to figure out what that purpose is.

Once I was teaching a workshop to some government employees and talking about destiny, when suddenly a woman in the audience yelled, "Oh, I get it!" The group seemed amused and intrigued, so I invited the woman to share her moment of illumination.

"I just realized now why I am so stressed out in my life," she said. "It's because I'm whatless."

"Whatless?" I inquired.

"Yeah, I have no *what*, no destiny, no purpose and no meaning." As she finished explaining, quiet descended on the group.

She had touched a nerve. She had pinpointed a source of angst for many people.

It's stressful to be without a destination. Imagine getting in your car but not knowing where you're going. Imagine boarding a plane, but the airline hasn't told you where the flight is headed. That's crazy. How will you know what to pack or how to plan for your trip? Yet that's how many of us live our lives.

Picture yourself adrift in a fast-flowing river (wearing a life-preserver, of course). The river represents change. The river's current is constantly moving you, crashing you into rocks, rushing you past fallen trees and large boulders. You feel powerless. Every now and then you pass by a place that intrigues you. You would like to tell the river to stop, to let you off so that you can explore the place further and discover the gifts that might be waiting for you. But the river doesn't listen. It has its own agenda, and you, after all, are only along for the ride.

So many of us believe in the glory of the afterlife, yet we have no clear vision of what we want in *this* life. I've read that most people spend more time thinking about and planning a one-week vacation than they do their whole lives. It's great that we can, for the most part, take one day at a time. But it's sad that so many people have no idea of who they are or what their destiny is. We're drifters. We're not connected to what makes us truly great and truly unique. We don't set goals. We let our dreams die.

Your *what*—your mission, vision, vocation, calling, bliss, meaning, destiny—won't come from reading a book or taking a workshop. There's no such thing as a hand-me-down destiny. You must create it from scratch, like good bread. It comes from the well of passion deep within you. It takes time and work to get to your authentic Essence, your precious core. The journey to find your destiny is the journey to find your Self. To cross your bridge, you must become something of a spiritual warrior.

Spiritual warriors want to connect with something greater than themselves. They thirst for meaning and clarity. They want to understand their purpose—why they're here.

Why are you here? What is your life about? What's important to you?

YOUR VALUES: WHAT WOULDN'T YOU SACRIFICE?

Often people attempt to live their lives backwards: they try to have more things, or more money, in order to do more of what they want so that they will be happier. The way it actually works is the reverse. You must first be who you really are, then, do what you need to do, in order to have what you want.

—MARGARET YOUNG

Nelson Mandela refused to sacrifice his freedom. He worked hard to bring an end to racial injustice in South Africa. His fight landed him in prison, where he spent twenty-seven years. He suffered unrelenting isolation and hard labor, but he did not break. Eventually, after his release from prison and following reconciliation with then-president F W de Klerk, a democratic election was held. During a historic four days in 1994, millions of blacks across South Africa exercised their right to vote—a right they had never had before, and for which Mandela had risked his life.

Freedom. That's what we think of when we hear the name Nelson Mandela. What wouldn't you sacrifice? In other words, what is sacred to you? What matters most? What values do you hold dear? What priorities do you live by?

Your values are a compass for your life. I love the symbol of the compass, because today most of us badly need one. We're not aligned with what is most important to us. We don't walk our talk. We say family is important, and yet, day after day and week after week, we put family time on the back burner while our work takes priority. We make excuses. We compromise. We say that good health and exercise are important, but every day we eat junk food in front of the TV. We say we're committed to our faith, our spiritual journey, and yet we haven't learned to really go within and listen to God. We say we want to keep learning and stay current, but we don't seem to have the time. We seek balance, but we falter. So we sacrifice our ideals and our values.

THE IMPORTANCE OF COMPASS

> Imagine life as a game in which you are juggling five
> balls . . . work, family, health, friends, and spirit.
> Work is a rubber ball. If you drop it, it will bounce back.
> But the other four balls are made of glass. If you drop
> one of these, they will never be the same.
>
> —BRIAN DYSON

Knowing what your compass is and how to align your choices and actions with it are the key ingredients for living a happy and fulfilled life. So much of our frustrations and stress arise from incongruity—incongruity between what we think, feel, and say is important and how we actually spend our time. For example, I'll ask people, "What's most important to you?" Most will list family as their highest priority, but when they look at how they spend their time, family is usually at the bottom. Our values don't match our actions. Perhaps what's needed is a values-clarification exercise, or learning to say no to the unimportant things. You must let your compass be your guide.

I first started teaching people the importance of compass after reading the ideas of Stephen Covey. No one does a better job of showing us how we have been leading incongruent lives. It's not just individuals who are ignorant of their internal compass; companies, governments, and organizations are lost as well. Leadership today is about giving a team a clear vision, mandate, purpose, destination—in short, a compass. Aligning effort with compass produces results: Everyone is on the same page and communication flows. The end is achieved.

Compass is also important for personal time management. For so many of us, time management remains the last frontier. We can do everything but manage our schedules and cope with the ever-increasing to-do list. After Covey published *The Seven Habits of Highly Effective People,* his organization did a survey to find out which habit people had the most difficulty with, which habit was toughest to live? The survey found that it was Habit 3: "Put first things first"—in other words, time management.

I think the reason people can't put first things first is because they don't know what their "first things" are. This idea has been reinforced by the many workshops and seminars I have delivered. When we look at the clock, we know that we must move our feet, but where will we go? Compass tells us where.

If we don't have a compass, we do what most people do—go in circles, become distracted, procrastinate, or waste time on the unimportant. We ignore the priorities of our lives because they are not clearly defined, or we lack the motivation to be true to them. Compass tells us what these priorities are. I have found that when it comes to our individual lives, most of us need to reacquaint ourselves with our compass. We knew what was important once, but the river of life has taken us downstream, far from our bliss, far from what's important to us. We need to make the journey back home. We need to realign our lives.

How to Align Your Life

**When we do what matters most,
we are not at the mercy of what matters least.**
—STEPHEN COVEY

STEP 1: CHOOSE YOUR CORE VALUES

The following is a list of values. Take out your journal and think about them. Which ones are most significant to you? Choose your top ten. If you have a value that is not on the list, add it.

Love	Loyalty	Meaning	Wisdom	Education
Family	Spirituality	Money	Service	Friendship
Security	Creativity	Health	Career	Pleasure
Joy	Honesty	Environment	Altruism	Achievement
Faith	Beauty	Humility	Playfulness	Growth
Balance	Religion	Courage	Compassion	Adventure
Music	Freedom	Status	Solitude	Fun

STEP 2: PRIORITIZE YOUR VALUES

Now put your top ten in order from most important to least important. Number them by assigning your most important value a 1 and the least important a 10.

STEP 3: GIVE YOURSELF A SCORE

Look at your top five values. Now grade yourself according to how well you have lived out that value in the past month. For example, if you chose Family as one of your top five values, ask

55

yourself, "In the past month, has my behavior reflected this value?" If not, how should you behave in order to live this value? To some people, quantity of time is important. To others, it's more the quality of fun, laughter, and connection with a family member. Whatever it means for you to live that value, how well did you do in the past month? How true have you been to this value? Write this down: "In the past month I have been able to live this value _____ percent of the time." Now, do this for each of the top five values you chose.

STEP 4: EVALUATE YOUR VALUES

Look at your least important five values and perhaps even the ones that didn't make your list. Are you devoting time to these lesser values? If so, why? Do you need to say no? Do you need to stop procrastinating? Do you need a wake-up call? For example, let's say you listed Service as number 10, but you notice that in the past month much of your time has been spent sitting on committees, going to meetings, and doing volunteer work— at the expense of your top values. Ask yourself, "Why am I being distracted from my top values?"

I find that this step allows for introspection. People ask themselves questions they've never asked before. For example, "Where did I get this value? Is it really my value, or did I inherit it from my parents or my culture?" Alignment happens when your values match the convictions of your authentic Self.

STEP 5: IDENTIFY ACTION STEPS

Beside each value, identify one thing that you can do—one action step—that will help you align yourself with the priority that value has in your life. For example, if Health is number 2, identify one action step you can take that will take you closer to that value. You might say you will go for a walk at lunch, get more sleep, or avoid deep-fried foods. If you can identify more than one action step that will bring you closer to your value, so much the better.

There are times when you have to say no so that you can give your energy and time to your top priorities. There are only twenty-four hours in a day. I know that most of us need far more than that to get everything done. Our lives are busy most of the time. But life is about making choices. When we don't live according to our values, we're living according to someone else's values. We lose our integrity. When our actions are incongruent with our values, we're not in control of our destiny. We are adrift in the river. Our souls become polluted; our spirits sag; our lives are out of alignment. It's time for you to take out your compass and decide what's most important to you, right now. It's time for you to create your personal destiny mandala.

CREATE YOUR PERSONAL DESTINY MANDALA

Our lives are works in progress.
—SUSAN L. TAYLOR

So how do we find out our destiny? How can we know what we were born to do? The answers are within you. When you connect deeply with each compass direction, you gain insight into your destiny, purpose, or mission. Creating a destiny mandala is an opportunity for self-discovery and personal reflection.

The North represents your spiritual dimension. It's the North Star in the night sky that helps lost travelers to find their way.

Your Spirit is like the North Star. When you feel overwhelmed by what life sends you, you need to connect to your Source, your Creator, and get spiritually nourished. You need to be reminded of what is sacred to you.

The South represents your intellectual faculties, the vast power of your mind. This is the area of knowledge, wisdom, and information. Life is a school. What did you come here to learn?

I've chosen the East to represent the realm of the emotions—east is where the sun rises and where possibilities are born. Within us, possibilities are born in our hearts. We must feel them, become passionate, and then move our mountains.

The West represents our physical body. The West is the final frontier. It's for brave hearts who keep pushing forward. You need endurance to go West. You need courage to push your body's physical threshold.

Each cardinal point poses questions that you need to answer to complete the destiny mandala. The destiny mandala is meant to be a visual guide, a map reminding you of who you are and what's important to you in every aspect of your life. You might have to dig deep and become vulnerable in order to answer some of the questions that will arise. I encourage you to draw your destiny mandala on a large sheet of paper and answer your questions on it. Each direction can be a different color—be creative.

Your answers can be one word or a paragraph long. There are no right or wrong answers.

NORTH: SPIRITUAL COMPASS

- Who am I?
- What is sacred to me?

Destiny Mandala

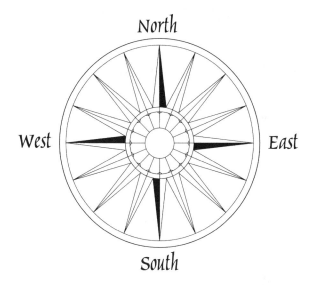

- What did I come here to do?
- How does God/the Universe/the Beloved speak to me?
- How can I make the world a better place with my spiritual gifts?
- What spiritual "undones" do I have?
- What symbol expresses my true spiritual Self?

SOUTH: INTELLECTUAL COMPASS

- What did I come here to learn?
- What did I come here to unlearn?
- What/who did I come here to teach?
- What are my intellectual gifts?

- How can I make the world a better place with my intellectual gifts?
- What intellectual "undones" do I have?
- What symbol expresses my intellectual gifts?

EAST: EMOTIONAL COMPASS

- Who did I come here to love?
- Who did I come here to forgive?
- What brings my heart joy?
- What did I come here to heal?
- How can I make the world a better place with my emotional gifts?
- What emotional "undones" do I have?
- What symbol best represents my emotional gifts?

WEST: PHYSICAL COMPASS

- What part of my body needs healing?
- What part of my body needs acceptance/nurturing/care?
- How can I be kinder to my body?
- How does my body want to express itself?
- How can I make the world a better place with my physical gifts?
- What physical "undones" do I have?
- What symbol represents my body and my physical gifts?

EXAMPLES

John's North compass (spiritual):
1 *Who am I?* Sacred, funny, loving, magnificent.

2 *What is sacred to me?* Love, connection, meaning, synchronicities, God.

3 *What did I come here to do?* To help others heal.

4 *How does God/the Universe/the Beloved speak to me?* Through my feelings.

5 *How can I make the world a better place with my spiritual gifts?* Teach people about love and faith.

6 *What spiritual "undones" do I have?* Learn to meditate. Develop my psychic abilities.

7 *What symbol expresses my true spiritual self?* A kaleidoscope.

Kate's East compass (emotional):

1 *Who did I come here to love?* Myself.

2 *Who did I come here to forgive?* Those in the dark.

3 *What brings my heart joy?* Love, flowers, springtime, little children.

4 *What did I come here to heal?* Myself, my past.

5 *How can I make the world a better place with my emotional gifts?* Teach people to wake up and be passionate.

6 *What emotional "undones" do I have?* Forgiving those I know I must forgive.

7 *What symbol best represents my emotional gifts?* An angel.

After you have finished creating your destiny mandala, study it. Observe patterns. What words or ideas come up more than once? Your destiny mandala is a way for you to reaffirm what is most important to you and what you came here to do. It's a tool for self-celebration and self-actualization. The more aligned you are with what is sacred to you, the more likely you are to take action towards that end. Preparing a destiny mandala lays the groundwork for your life's mission statement.

A MISSION STATEMENT EXERCISE

**You are either living your mission,
or you are living someone else's.**
—LAURIE BETH JONES

The word "mission" comes from the Latin *missio*, which means "sending." It can also mean "special vocation or calling"—as in "Medicine was her mission"—which can be associated with your career or life's work. The question here is: Where are you "sending" your life? To what destination?

Companies post mission statements or corporate values in their lobbies or boardrooms. These tell customers and remind employees what the company stands for. But mission statements are not only for companies and organizations. They're for individuals and families, too. A personal mission statement tells the world what you stand for, what your gifts are, and how you want to make a difference. It describes your unique purpose and how you want to be living your life. Because you are unique, your personal mission statement will be unlike anyone else's.

Stephen Covey says that a personal mission statement "becomes a personal constitution, the basis for making major, life-directing decisions, the basis for making daily decisions in the midst of the circumstances and emotions that affect our lives."[1]

Your mission is what helps you take the step every day. It's the destination on the other side of the bridge. If you have a mission, then you are not "whatless"; you know where your life is to go. That's because it represents a vision, a destination, a purpose. And when you wake up with a vision, destination, and purpose every morning, you can't help but bring your soul to work. You will cure the spiritual malaise that is prevalent in so many lives today.

The faster the river of change, the easier it is to get distracted. Why do we do the things we do every day? Why do we chase the wrong things? Have we lost perspective? Have we sold out our moral principles? A mission statement brings you back on course. It's the compass when you're lost at sea.

There are different schools of thought as to how to write a mission statement and how long it should be. After all, why is it called a statement if some people need to use several paragraphs? There are no hard and fast rules. If your mission statement is a song lyric, so be it, as long as it speaks to you and gives you a sense of calling. I heard of a man whose mission statement was "I want to be the kind of person my dog already thinks I am." That's short and to the point. A client of mine once told me her mission was Love. That's it—one word.

Richard Bolles says in *How to Find Your Mission in Life* that we all have three missions. They are:

- To know God
- To make this world a better place
- To exercise the talent that is uniquely yours

He says the first two missions are shared with others. The last one is unique to you.

You can cull information and inspiration from all kinds of sources, including your destiny mandala and the passion exercises you will do in chapter 3, to come up with something that is uniquely yours. Most people's mission statements talk about what they are going to do according to what's important to them. Philosopher Victor Frankl says we detect rather than invent our missions in life. If we have a special vocation or purpose, then we must stay alert to the *calls* our souls send us. We must pay attention.

There are many ways in which you can write a mission statement. Here is one way:

Step 1: The first part of the mission statement is information about you. Who are you? Say a journalist from another galaxy has arrived to interview you. What adjectives best describe your unique qualities, talents, and gifts? Here are some examples:

- I am a beautiful, kind, articulate, passionate, and sensitive person.
- I am an intelligent, original, inspirational, compassionate, and powerful person.
- I am a gutsy, raw, artistic, creative, reflective, and soulful person.

Step 2: What do you want to contribute? Talk about what you want to do for the world. How do you want to make a difference? Look at your destiny mandala. What brings you joy? What are you passionate about? What did you learn about yourself when you answered the mandala questions? Here are some examples:

- My mission is to acknowledge the sacred in all people and all things.
- My mission is to inspire, love, and empower people so they can create the highest vision of who they are.

- My mission is to educate the world about conservation and protection of our planet.
- My mission is to help people in the Third World.

Step 3: Combine Parts 1 and 2 together. For example:

- I am a beautiful, kind, passionate, sensitive, and soulful person whose mission is to acknowledge the sacred in all people and all things.
- I am an enthusiastic, courageous, intelligent, and adventurous person whose mission is to teach children how to take care of our planet.

You can spend hours—even days—on your mission statement trying to get the words to flow. Don't become frustrated. Focus on the ideas. Don't worry about poetry or eloquence. The right words will evolve as you revisit it.

If your mission statement still won't come, just sit and reflect for a while. You may need to let the wisdom of your unconscious mind percolate to the surface. When you have a statement that rings true, say it to yourself often. Try it out loud. Post it where you're likely to see it daily. Some great places are on a bulletin board in front of your workspace, on the first page of your agenda, or on your refrigerator. Try it as a screen saver even.

Your mission statement becomes your overall compass. It is the direction in which you want to move your life. Your compass represents all that is meaningful and sacred to you. Living your life "on purpose" means you're living in accordance with your mission statement.

CONTEMPLATING OUR MORTALITY

**The midlife crisis . . . probably reflects the fact
that at midlife one's own death becomes less theoretical
and more probable.**
—ARTHUR J. DEIKMAN

In his bestseller *Tuesdays with Morrie*, Mitch Albom writes about
his visits to his old college professor, Morrie Schwartz, who is
dying of Lou Gehrig's disease, a brutal neurological disorder.
As Morrie gets progressively worse, Mitch visits him every
Tuesday and they have wonderful conversations about life. One
week, when Mitch asks him about death, Morrie recommends
that we imitate the Buddhists and be prepared for death at any
time. The reason? So we can be more involved in our lives while
we're living them.

"The truth is, Mitch," he tells his student, "once you learn
how to die, you learn how to live."[2] Morrie's words are wise. It's
only when we contemplate our mortality that we know how we
want to live. It's only by contemplating our death that we feel
the need to squeeze every last bit of joy out of our life. Morrie
says that the reason we don't focus on our death more often is
because we're all sleepwalking, living our lives by habit, not by
intention. If you were told you had only one year to live, would
you see things differently? Would you stop postponing your life
and start taking action? How do you want to make a difference?
How do you want to be remembered?

WHAT WILL THEY SAY AFTER YOU'RE GONE?

All that is real in our past is the love we gave and the love we received. Everything else is an illusion.

—MARIANNE WILLIAMSON

One of the most poignant exercises I've ever done was to write down what I wanted people to say at my funeral. These are the sentiments you would want people to express about you after you're gone. While our children were visiting their grandparents, my husband and I both sat down to visit with our destiny. It was New Year's Eve, 1999, the close of one millennium and the dawn of a new one. It was time to realign my life.

I focused on what I wanted my friends and family to say about me after my death. What celebration statements would they offer? How would they evaluate my life? When I got to my children, I was overcome with emotion. I found myself asking, "What kind of mother do I want to be? How do I want to influence their lives?" With tears in my eyes, I wrote, "She showed me kindness, compassion, and unconditional love. She inspired me to reach for the stars. I am the person I am today because of my mother's love."

What did I want my friends to say? "Grace was a true friend. She believed in me and loved me, and always inspired me to look for the best in myself and others. She was an angel of compassion—that's why God sent her to us."

What did I want my clients to say? "Grace Cirocco inspired me to *just do it!* She taught me how to live life to the fullest and go for my dreams. Her passion for life and her love for all people means we are all richer just to have known her."

The underlying question in the exercise is this: If that's what

I want each person to say about me, then what do I have to do every day to get there? In other words, what actions, what steps must I take to get those results?

Admitting to myself that this was the legacy I wanted to leave behind was a powerful exercise for me. I now had a clear path ahead. I revisited my mission statement and wrote down my goals. I needed to know where I was going to "send" my life in the new millennium. When it comes to the most important relationships in your life, doing an exercise like this will help you decide what is on the other side of your bridge—what you're working towards. Once you figure out your *what* in each relationship, it's easier to take action.

Sometimes you need to contemplate your death so you can reprioritize your life. Do you have a birthday coming up? Are summer holidays around the corner? Perhaps New Year's Eve? If not, any day will do. Make yourself a pot of tea, put on your most comfortable clothes, sit in your favorite chair, open your journal, or take out your laptop. Decide what you want people to say about you when you're gone.

LISTENING TO THE CALL OF YOUR SOUL

**The heroic life is living the individual adventure.
To refuse the call means stagnation.**
—JOSEPH CAMPBELL

Another way to gain clarity about your destiny is to listen to the call of your soul. When your soul speaks, it is felt in the heart. So what is this "call of the soul," and how do you know whether you've experienced it? A calling is similar to a mission or purpose, but it is more general. For example, you may feel a calling to do community work; when you investigate the contributions you can make, you realize that what you really want is to help the disabled become more self-sufficient. This becomes your mission, or destiny, but you wouldn't have found it had you not listened to that original feeling, the "call."

When you actively listen to your soul's calling, you are also listening to God. Your calling is the voice of intuition that gently urges you to see what possibilities you can manifest in your life. When you pay attention to that inner hunch that says "follow this passion" or "talk to that person" or "read that book," you are honoring your soul—you are surrendering your life to a higher Power. The soul calls us to express our creativity and our unique gifts. It is a tug from the future, pulling you towards limitless possibilities and endless potential.

I think we can feel this call about many things in a lifetime. Sometimes it is a whisper, a subtle tug at the heart that says "I want to know more" or "I like this." Sometimes it's very loud. It hits us over the head with a hammer and doesn't let us sleep, eat, or function until we pay attention.

No one really knows the origin of this call. It comes from your soul, yes, but why this call and not another one? Why was I called to inspire and empower people on how to live more meaningful lives and not, for example, how to maximize their investments? Because the former mission is part of my destiny and the latter is not. The soul knows its destiny and wants us to live it out. And so it helps us. It gives us messages, yearnings, warnings, and feelings that will eventually lead us to that destiny. Some people are good at hearing the call; others are not. The more conscious you are, the more connected you feel to your Creator and to your authentic Self, the greater your ability to recognize the call when it comes.

Sometimes we get the call when we are children. One of my clients got the call to be a marine biologist and dolphin trainer when as a child he saw his first dolphins on a trip to Florida. He was smitten, he says. He knew right then and there that he wanted to learn everything he could about these magnificent creatures.

In one lifetime we may have several callings that point us in the direction our soul needs to go. We can experience callings about our work, our careers, our education, our surroundings (where we need to live or travel to), our relationships, and our spiritual mission. The call from the soul doesn't have to be a final destination. In many cases, it is only leading us towards our mission or destiny. Sometimes several calls are components of one mission. Sometimes a call may be a steppingstone, something you need to learn before you can fulfill your life's work.

I was once invited to be on a television program where people could phone in with their questions. One person asked me how he could distinguish between a calling and a fantasy? Good question. He said that his fantasy was to live by the ocean.

"So what's stopping you?" I asked him.

"It's not realistic," he said. "We both have jobs here, plus we just bought a house."

I told him that this yearning was like a call from his soul. He might call it a fantasy, but the fantasy was calling his name. Sometimes the call from the soul may have nothing to do with your vocation, but everything to do with your happiness. If you're happy with your surroundings, you'll be happier with your life, and the happiness will spill over into other areas of life as well. Wanting to live by the ocean may not be a vocation, but it can certainly be a call from the soul. Sometimes a fantasy is an image built up of what we think it will be or what we want it to be. Perhaps we call it a fantasy because we do not truly believe we can achieve it.

A calling, on the other hand, is felt in the heart. Sometimes callings are not logical. Just when we think we have our lives in order, our soul grows restless and begins to grumble. It hands us something right out of the clear blue sky. We think, "This can't possibly be real. Look at my life. I'm organized. Everything is set. I'm happy. Aren't I?"

THE CALL THAT COMES WITH ENTHUSIASM

**Years wrinkle the skin, but to give up
enthusiasm wrinkles the soul.**

—SAMUEL ULLMAN

There were two hundred women in the large hotel conference room. Our seminar leader was talking about how we all have our own communication style. It was a professional seminar—my first—and suddenly I got "the call." Actually, it was more like a lightning bolt. That whole day I kept thinking, "This is it! This is what I want to do when I grow up." I could barely contain my enthusiasm.

I went home and told my husband. Three weeks later I was competing with more than five hundred other hopefuls in a hotel ballroom. We were there because of an ad in the newspaper: "International seminar company looking for seminar leaders to expand its business." There was no telephone number, just the location, time, and date.

I had recently given birth to my daughter, Kajsa, and was still nursing her, so I could not leave her alone for more than a couple of hours. The meeting was at least an hour away. How was I going to do this? How was I going to balance the call of my soul with motherhood? (There are women who face this challenge on a daily basis!) My husband, always prepared to support my call (bless his heart) came through with a solution. "Let's all go together. I'll wait in the lobby with the kids. That way, if Kajsa gets hungry, you're close by."

Everything I heard during the presentation made me even more excited. "Yup, yup, yup," my soul was saying, "this is for you, Grace." When the meeting was over, we were invited to come back the next morning and audition on videotape. "Speak about what you know," the interviewer said. Those were the only instructions we got. I was a broadcast journalist, so I knew about writing for the ear, and that's what I talked about.

It took the company several months to go through all the tapes and make a decision, but eventually they short-listed six candidates to undergo train-the-trainer training. I was one of those six. Although we had been selected to be trained, we were told not to assume that we would get the job. It was just another part of the selection process.

After the training, I got the phone call that invited me to join their team. I was one of two candidates to be hired. I was thrilled. I had been true to my calling and now the Universe was rewarding me. My life and career took a dramatic shift. I was getting closer to my mission. As soon as you figure out your "what," the Universe will deliver the "how"—the logistics of how it will manifest in your life. I see this pattern repeating itself in the lives of many of my friends and clients.

The piano has eighty-eight keys. It occurs to me that before we die, our job is to play our song on all eighty-eight keys. Earlier in my life I had received the call to be a broadcast journalist. I wrote, edited, and produced newscasts and current affairs programming. I was good at it. I liked it. But I wasn't playing my song with all eighty-eight keys; on good days, I used maybe sixty. As a speaker, teacher, coach, counselor, and now writer, I feel I am finally playing my song with eighty-eight keys—perhaps not every single day, but I know I have used them all. I consider that a privilege.

When your work is in line with your calling, it doesn't seem like work. Everything flows. You feel exhilarated, excited by the next possibility. You're empowered, and things happen as if by magic. Some of us get the call for meaningful work (using all eighty-eight keys) as a child, like my client who knew he'd be working with dolphins. For others, like me, it's a cumulative process. Each call that we pay attention to and act on lays a foundation for recognizing the call that will have us playing on the whole keyboard. When was the last time you heard your song played with all eighty-eight keys?

One way to know that you're getting close to the eighty-eight keys is to gauge how enthusiastic you are about something. The root of enthusiasm, *entheos*, is Greek and means "filled with God." When we're filled with God, we're also filled with soul. Enthusiasm is, therefore, the language of our soul, and the language of the soul is energy. When energy speaks to you, you need to listen—your soul's calling may be close by. This enthusiasm can be for anything. If you're enthusiastic about a career, a branch of knowledge, an idea, a place, a book, a song, or a person, pay attention to it. It's your soul's way of telling you that your eighty-eight keys may be on the next page of the music book.

THE CALL THAT WON'T LEAVE US ALONE

Is that what they call a vocation, what you do with joy as if you had fire in your heart, the devil in your body?
—JOSEPHINE BAKER

His name is Brother Andre, my husband tells me, and he performs miracles. He heals people. My husband, Santo, heard about the healing miracles of Brother Andre through a friend who had been cured of a back problem that had kept him in bed for ten years. Brother Andre had spent time in prison for crimes related to drug and alcohol abuse. He was not your typical miracle worker, but he finally had to listen to the unusual call he kept getting. He was seeing visions of Mother Mary, who would come to him while he was sleeping. Sometimes he'd open his eyes and there she was in his bedroom, telling him that he was to heal people, that he had special powers to help the sick. He was terrified that he was going crazy and for two years completely denied the visions. He kept insisting that she had the wrong guy, but the call from the Virgin Mother was persistent.

Eventually Brother Andre gave in. Today there are people who feel they owe their lives to this man. He is playing his song with all eighty-eight keys. His compass and his mission have made him a modern-day healer empowered to perform miracles. I don't understand how it works. I do know that amazing things can happen if you have faith. Whether the healing miracles happen because of Brother Andre or because of people's faith in his powers, it's not important. What is important is that he eventually had the courage to heed the call that wouldn't go away. He has done a lot of good in the world by visiting and healing the sick. Because he listened to his special call, Brother Andre lives his unique mission every day.

Sometimes people will ignore the call. Rita, a client of mine who is in her fifties, is sad that she didn't have the courage to listen to her heart when she was younger. When she was in her early teens, she knew she wanted to become a Roman Catholic nun. From the beginning, she had been a missionary, wanting to bring people to Christ. When Rita mentioned this career choice to her parents, they flipped out, she says. Too afraid of losing their love and acceptance, Rita sold out her soul's longing for

something her parents approved of, eventually enrolling in sec-
retarial college.

For most of her life, Rita felt lost. She had denied who she was
in order to make her parents happy, and for many years she
drifted in and out of jobs and relationships. Today she feels
more in control of her life because she met and married a man
who's something of a missionary himself. They volunteer at
their church and in the community, speaking of Jesus to whoever will listen. Even though she didn't become a nun, she says
she's happy now. There are many ways to manifest our calling.
And it's never too late.

TAKING STEPS TOWARDS YOUR GOALS

A journey of a thousand leagues begins with a single step.
—LAO-TZU

Many of us don't take action because our path is not clearly laid
out. The secret is this: Make a plan. Write down the baby-steps
you must take to listen to the call from your soul or accomplish
a goal. Brainstorm. The best way to do that is to draw a goal
map (see page 77). Write your goal or vision—the final end
result (what you want) in the middle of a circle and then draw
spokes radiating from the circle. Write your ideas on the spokes.
Once you have your ideas written down, prioritize each step.
Ask yourself, "What do I need to do first?" Make a list of the
necessary steps and assign yourself a deadline.

Each week, schedule one or two things in your agenda that
will move you towards your goal. This is effective goal-setting.
Life is just like this—a series of small steps. Sometimes we are
paralyzed with fear because the thing we want to do overwhelms

us. Break this fear down, tackle one element at a time, and soon you'll be across the bridge.

Another thing you can do (and this is important) is regularly visualize the goal *as if it has already happened.* This is the secret to success. Thinking *of* the goal is not enough. You must think *from* your goal. You must put yourself in the goal and visualize yourself having, being, or doing the thing you want. So if you really want to go on a world cruise, go there in your mind first. Imagine the ship you're on; imagine the countries you visit. Make a multi-sensory movie inside your mind about how it would feel, look, taste, and sound. More about this very powerful tool in chapter 5.

Goal-setting is a habit of highly effective people. They don't get discouraged. Rather, they plug away at their dreams every day while balancing their job and family obligations. Rome wasn't built overnight, and neither will be your dreams. Consistent action taken over time will give you the results you want.

After doing the exercises in this chapter, if you still don't have a clear idea of what is waiting for you on the other side of the bridge, consider goals in the following categories:

- personal growth and development
- career/work
- adventure/travel/fun
- family/friends
- your spiritual journey
- your legacy (how you want to make a difference)

Choose one category and then ask, "What do I want?" Start working on that goal.

Creating a Goal Map

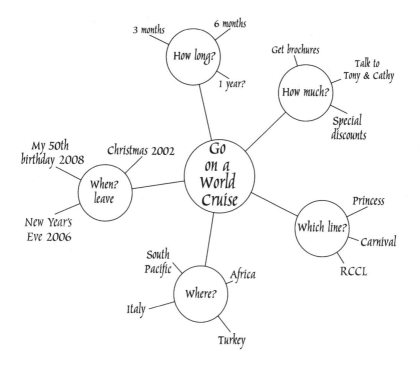

Prioritize the steps: what do you need to do first?

To achieve your goals, consider the following tips:

- Write your goals down and post them where you will see them (some of these can be your affirmations).
- Use active verbs, not the passive voice.
- Use the present continuous tense (for example, "I am attracting . . ." rather than "I will attract . . .").

- Be specific: What? When? How much? Who?
- Dream big—accept no limitations.
- Visualize, visualize, visualize the end-result of your vision on a daily basis.
- Create a self-fulfilling prophecy: Expect success from yourself.

3

Awaken Your
Passion

A PASSION FOR LIFE

**One has to abandon altogether the search for security and
reach out to the risk of living with both arms. We need to
embrace the world like a lover.**

—MORRIS L. WEST

What makes your heart beat more quickly? What makes your
eyes shine and every cell in your body feel electrified? When
was the last time you embraced the world like a lover? Passion
is the stuff of dreams. It can be hot, intense, colorful. It brings
texture and meaning to life. It is the antidote to depression. It
keeps you alive and in the joy of the moment. Passion is a pul-
sating energy that keeps you connected to your own life force,
to your purpose, and to the universal Intelligence present in
nature. Passion is the fuel of artists, poets, and those who thirst
for a more meaningful journey. Passion ignites the soul. Passion
is courage that propels us forward across the bridge. Without

passion for life, getting out of bed in the morning would be a meaningless experience.

Passion is much more than the sexual feelings we have for a lover. Remembering the life and death of Princess Diana, Sarah Ban Breathnach explained passion's broader meaning: "Passion is color; most of us live in black and white. For me Diana's great gift was that she was willing to embrace her passion, to attempt to live authentically. . . . If Diana's death imparts only one lesson, it is that passion is holy, to be embraced, even if we tremble with fear."[1]

Passionate people are committed. They follow through. You cannot be both passionate and self-contained. Passion wants to burst forth, to fly up and be noticed. It wants to express itself in creative ways.

The enemy of passion is fear. Why don't we take the step towards our heart's longing? Because we're afraid. If we could connect to our passion, find its source deep within us, we could also learn to start taking small steps towards what is meaningful and sacred to us. Passion is the solution for so much of the malaise we feel—and yet we ignore it. Why?

WHY DO WE PUT OUT THE FLAME OF PASSION?

Passion lops off the bough of weariness. Passion is the elixir that renews. . . . Oh, don't sigh heavily from fatigue: seek passion, seek passion, seek passion!

—RUMI

I think we have been trying to put out the flame of passion for hundreds of years. A genre of books and films that has always fascinated me explores the sanity/insanity issue. The main characters in the films *One Flew Over the Cuckoo's Nest, Mr. Jones,* and *Man Facing Southeast,* for example, are deemed crazy by the outside world. But to me, they personify passion in its highest form. These are heroes who take risks and live on the edge. They can't be classified as "normal," because they get too excited about life and wear their passions on their sleeves. They live life at full throttle.

In both *Mr. Jones* and *Man Facing Southeast,* there is a scene where the main character loses control while listening to Beethoven's Ninth Symphony. He is so filled with music that he stands up and starts conducting from his seat (obviously, this distracts the other patrons). Eventually, unable to contain his joy, he walks on stage and tries to lead the orchestra, much to the shock of the conductor, who is only trying to do his job. "Normal" people don't do this. Both characters break the rules. The verdict? They must be crazy, so in both films the police arrive and take them away. It seems there is a fine line between being passionate and being crazy, between insanity and being high on life.

When we can't tame passion, we amputate it. It starts in childhood. So many of us were raised by controlling parents who wanted to choose our clothes, our music, and our friends. If you flew too high, or even imagined you had wings, you'd soon find them clipped, maimed, or worse, plucked out. I think I was too much for my poor mother. She didn't know what to do with such an intense child, her daughter who was so outrageously passionate about life. She tried her best to stamp out my "craziness" and make me conform to her idea of what a nice girl should be—but I had my own ideas. There were adventures I wanted to experience, places I wanted to see, and things I wanted to do. I refused to follow anyone's path, especially not the path prescribed for girls by my Italian heritage. That made me "different" and "difficult."

I think my mother was frightened that my passion would one day get me in trouble. She was worried about me, but by the time I reached adulthood, she had become resigned to my iconoclastic ways. I think she finally grew to understand me because she could remember a time when she too had the passion stamped out of her.

The question is "why"? I believe it's because passion is threatening.

Marianne Williamson, in her book *A Woman's Worth*, remembers how fond she was of "Betty Lynn," the glamorous woman who lived across the street when she was a child. Betty Lynn was outrageous and drove a champagne-colored Cadillac. She always had a drink in her hand, and it was alcohol that eventually killed her. Williamson writes, "Why do people who have the most ardor, the most enchantment, the most power, so often feel the need for drugs and alcohol? They do not drink just to dull their pain; they drink to dull their ecstasy. . . . Betty Lynn crucified herself before anyone else had a chance to."[2]

It's true. Sometimes it seems like the world is not ready for our passion, our high-octane Spirit. So we apologize for it, hide it, or kill it. People may be jealous or scared that our passion will take something away from them. They're afraid of where passion might lead. It might break the rules and lead to change, and change is not always easy to embrace. Yes, there is still a lot of fear surrounding passion. This is the fault of a world that is still somewhat unenlightened, but the tide is turning. We're entering a new millennium, one that promises to embrace Spirit and, hopefully, celebrate passion. In the meantime, let's look at why passion is so difficult for some people to feel and show.

CHOOSING BETWEEN TWO PATHS

**I found out that I can do it, if I choose to—
I can stay awake and let the sorrows of the world tear
me apart and then allow the joys to put me back together,
different from before but whole again.**

—ORIAH MOUNTAIN DREAMER

I believe we have a choice in life to take one of two paths—the path of consciousness or the path of indifference. The path of consciousness is for spiritual warriors, for those committed to feeling passionate about life. They know that joy and sorrow are two sides of one coin, and they're not afraid to feel their feelings. The truth is that this path of consciousness was the starting point for all of us. We entered the world able to feel everything, experience everything, and respond to everything in the present moment. Some of us are still like that, childlike in our approach to the world. Trusting and loving, we put our hearts out there every day.

But for other people, the sorrows and betrayals of life have been too much to bear. Little by little, they shut down their emotions in an attempt to stop the pain. Others opt for complete anesthesia; they turn off their pain with drugs and alcohol. Some of us go shopping. There are many ways to "numb out."

Here's the unfortunate truth about this scenario: When you shut down the negative feelings—when you stop feeling—you also shut down the positive ones, like enthusiasm, love, joy, and passion. It's a little like taking antibiotics. The drugs destroy the bad bacteria in your body, but they also destroy the good bacteria. They are indiscriminate. That's why the more enlightened doctors these days recommend taking acidophilus as well as antibiotics in order to rebuild the good bacteria. Unfortunately, there is no equivalent to acidophilus for the Spirit. When we turn off the negative feelings, we turn off everything—the good, the bad, and the ugly feelings. We become numb. This is the path of indifference. We spend our days "putting in time," "surviving," and "getting by."

One of my favorite stories is told by author and motivational speaker Og Mandino in his book *The Greatest Miracle in the World*. His inspirational message is given via the hero of the story, Simon Potter, the wise ragpicker who comes out of nowhere, like some prophet or mystic, into the author's life. Simon reminds us that most people die at forty but are buried at eighty, and that the greatest miracle in the world is when people wake themselves up from a living death. "Pour the wine. You have been reborn. Like a butterfly from its chrysalis you will fly . . . and neither the wasps nor dragonflies nor mantids of mankind shall obstruct your mission."[3]

The cure for indifference is passion. Ask yourself, "Have I stopped caring? Feeling? Have I been taking the love, friendship, and kindness in my life for granted? Am I hiding behind a mask of indifference? Who am I running away from? Can I show my ecstasy?" Look at yourself and then look around you. Do you notice others who have opted for the path of indifference?

Barbara De Angelis, in her book *Passion*, says that some people try to excuse their indifference by masking it as spirituality, saying that they're practicing a form of detachment. De Angelis calls this "a kindergarten understanding of spiritual achievement."[4] In fact, she says, history reveals to us countless examples of saints, teachers, and holy beings who are the embodiment of passion and caring. The truth is that the holier we become, the more we feel for our fellow human beings. The more we feel, the more connected we are to our passion.

"Why should we grieve that we've been sleeping?" asks

Rumi, the Sufi poet. "It doesn't matter how long we've been unconscious. We're groggy, but let the guilt go."[5] Rumi is right. Let the guilt go. Focus on the future. Focus on waking up. Let's each take responsibility for choosing the conscious path, for being true to our passion, our authentic Self. How? By being aware of how we feel, by asking questions, by speaking the truth that is inside our hearts, by beating our own drum. Be interested in people when they talk to you—they have a gift for you. Be interested in the blade of grass, the sound of the wind, and the perfect blue of a robin's egg. They have gifts for you, too. The truth is that the Universe wants you to belong to it. It wants you to feel deeply the passion that beats in its core. Open your heart. Only then will your Spirit decide to get out of bed and join the human race. Only then will you be able to embrace the passion that is your birthright.

PSYCHIC ABSENCE

**My isolation was acute. . . . I wasn't dead. I wasn't alive.
I was suspended in a near-life experience.**
—SARAH BAN BREATHNACH

The woman cutting my daughter's hair was lifeless. There was a heaviness, an indescribable sadness about her. She dragged her feet. She didn't want to be there. I thought, "Perhaps it's her job. Perhaps she's suffered one too many rude and ungracious customers," and my heart went out to her. My daughter squealed with delight as her new, layered look came to life. As we left, we made a fuss over the stylist, letting everyone in the shop know how pleased we were. A faint smile flickered across her lips, but then it retreated. Driving home, I thought about her. I wondered whether she was grieving someone she loved or whether her indifference was a symptom that she was tired of her job, or perhaps tired of life. I wondered whether there was anything that brought her joy. I wanted to tell her she's beautiful, magnificent, and one hell of a hairdresser. I wanted to tell her that life is precious, and she has the power to create her life anew, regardless of what setbacks she may have suffered. Instead, I sent her a prayer that she might heal her heavy heart.

There are many reasons why we turn off. Some of us are grieving the death of a loved one, some of us can't cope with the challenges of life, some have lost the connection to their Source, some have unhealed wounds from the past, some are lonely and depressed, and some are just tired of everything. So we shut down. We opt for the path of indifference. We become psychically absent. We show up, but keep our souls in hiding. We do what we need to do, but we've lost the joy, the meaning of what life is all about.

Nowhere have I seen this lack of passion, this psychic absence, more than in the world of work, especially in the last ten years. One of the biggest problems today is a disengaged workforce. People get up in the morning and go to work, but they leave the best parts of themselves, their passion, their enthusiasm, and their creativity—in short, their Spirit—at home.

"My work is not about healing people anymore," a friend told me with sad resignation when we met for coffee the other day. "It's about dollars and cents." She sipped her latte and then stared off into the distance. "You know, Grace, I started working in the health profession because I cared. But those bastards have slowly sucked the blood out of me. I'm afraid I don't care anymore."

I've just heard that the husband of one of my clients, an engineer who for twenty years devoted himself to his organization, a multinational aeronautics company, has been fired. There was no warning and no compassion. Six senior people were called into the general manager's office and told that their services were no longer required. They were to empty their desks, collect their belongings, and leave with the security officer waiting to escort them off the premises.

These organizational brutalities happen all over the world. The sentiment expressed to me is always the same: "It's not what they did, but how they did it." Outplacement firms, career counselors, therapists, and coaches are still helping to pick up the pieces of those shattered lives.

A few years ago, I talked to hospital administrators who refused stress-management training for nurses during a difficult period of "re-engineering" because, according to them, "They're nurses—they should already know how to manage their stress!" While it's true that most of us know what to do, the problem is that many of us have been pushed to the limit in our workplaces, and our threshold for stress has been compromised. We're no longer resilient. We don't have the resources or the energy to bounce back. The result—no psychic energy.

Some experts believe that this psychically absent or disengaged workforce is largely the result of a top-down management approach. This management style *tells* people what to do. It belittles rather than engages the human Spirit. Top-down management is based on certain patriarchal beliefs that include (1) managers are smarter than everyone else, which is why most information flows downward; (2) people have to be controlled because, after all, they are a commodity; (3) business is a game; and (4) profit is how you keep score. These attitudes have not made it easy for the soul to come to work.

Another reason for psychic absence at work may be the lack

of trust that we feel in our professional relationships. "No one is really close any more," clients complain to me in coaching sessions. "Ever since the restructuring, trust is out the window." When there is no trust, there is no relationship. Betrayal is rampant. People grow apart; they stop talking. This alienation has been compounded by technology. Why go down the hall to speak to your boss or colleague when there's e-mail? Information flows from one person to another, but usually via a machine, not an organic being. If you don't feel connected to anyone at work, passion stays home.

THE UBIQUITOUS MORALE PROBLEM

In the end, indifference robs you of your greatest strength, your greatest protection. and your greatest blessing— the abundant love and passion that live in your heart.

—BARBARA DE ANGELIS

These days, employee motivation is a big issue. The most common request I get from organizational leaders is "Can you do something about the morale problem?" When people feel like commodities, unvalued and unappreciated, the human Spirit shuts down. Passion stays home. Our Light grows dim. We become numb. We produce mediocre results. Work is just a job, a means for paying bills.

If there is apathy in one part of our lives, it tends to spill over into other parts. Life is one indivisible whole. Many of us bring troubles from work home with us, whether we realize it or not, letting the stressors and negativity affect our personal lives. This psychic absence pervades every area of life. Some of us slip into depression, and we don't even know it. Depression is a disease that affects millions of people, and more every day. Millions of people are on antidepressants. We are dulling our senses in order to cope with a passionless world. Listen to how people talk about their work. "I can't believe it's Monday already!" "This job is killing me." "I can't wait until Friday." "I can't wait to get out of this place." "I've got five more years to go before retirement." Results from an annual Gallup poll showed that 80 percent of employees dread returning to work on Monday morning. The largest incidence of heart attacks and strokes is between 8 and 9 a.m. on Monday mornings. If it's time for your body to check out, why do it on a Friday when you have the weekend ahead?

The root of the word "employment" is the Latin word *implicare*, which means "to be involved." And being involved today means much more than security and a paycheck. Contrary to popular opinion, people go to work to feed their souls—to feel connected, to enhance self-worth, to learn, to have fun, and to contribute to something larger than themselves.

We need to change the focus and think about work as a contribution of our authentic gifts, as a vehicle for self-expression, as a way to align with our passion and purpose, and finally, as a vehicle for spiritual evolution and the healing of our planet. Some things need to change.

The good news is that things *are* changing. A spiritual awakening is happening—yes, even in the corporate world. Many organizational leaders I've worked with, in both the private and public sectors, not only believe in the physical, emotional, psychological, and even spiritual health of their staff, but they are also willing to invest in it. I'm always impressed by these brave hearts, as I call them, and their attitude gives me much to hope for. Robert Fritz, in his book *The Path of Least Resistance*, says

"The historic period in which we live is a period of reawakening to a commitment to higher values, a reawakening of individual purpose, and a reawakening of the longing to fulfill that purpose in life."[6] This reawakening of purpose is being spearheaded by spiritual warriors who are tuned into a higher frequency of consciousness. They are facilitating the path for Spirit in the workplace. They are committed to bringing more meaning and more passion to everyday life.

WHY DO YOU GO TO WORK?

When we work without passion, we quickly get burned out.
—BARBARA DE ANGELIS

Why do you go to work? Ask yourself that question. Make a list of all the reasons you go to work and then evaluate each reason. Is it an External Motivator (EM) or an Internal Motivator (IM)? External motivators are things like *pay my mortgage; send my kids to a private school; have a nice office; own a bigger home*, etc. Internal motivators are such things as *to contribute my talents; build friendships; help people; because it's my calling*.

Your reasons for doing the work you do are personal and unique to you. Your evaluations will depend on your filters and your interpretations. Don't get too hung up on whether you're interpreting a reason correctly. If you're having difficulty deciding whether it's an internal or external motivator, it's probably both. And that's okay.

To experience job/life satisfaction, we need to cultivate a balance between the external and internal motivators. If you're getting too many EMs, it could be that there is no joy keeping you in this job. It's just a means to an end. You may be psychically absent, taking only your body to work. If it's a temporary job situation, that's okay, but if not, think about making a change. You may have to do some soul-searching first. The exercises in chapter 2 and in this chapter will help you define and refine who you are and what gifts you have for the world. In the meantime, scan the horizon for additional opportunities. Make a plan.

If all you have are IMs, perhaps the job is running your life. You're out of balance. You get all your emotional needs met at work, so why have a personal life? People with only IMs eventually burn themselves out. I know all about this on a personal level.

As a producer for a radio current affairs program, I worked twelve-to-fourteen-hour days. But I didn't mind. I loved it and generated a lot of self-worth from my work. Then one night my husband came to the studio to bring me some food, and I couldn't get out of my chair. It was as if every single muscle in my body had locked. I spent two weeks in bed recovering from severe muscle spasms and had to take another month off work. I was physically burned out. When we love what we do, we're more likely to let the job take over our lives. Let the EMs and IMs open your eyes. To stay healthy, keep thinking *balance*.

TAKING OUR PASSION TO WORK

Passion doesn't come from business or books or even a connection with another person. It is a connection to your own life force, the world around you, and the spirit that connects us all. You are the source.
—JENNIFER JAMES

When Wayne Gretzky retired from playing hockey, he thanked God for giving him talent. Then he paused, thought about it, and said that it probably wasn't so much talent as it was the passion to play hockey. Without passion for our work, we lack the means for discovering our purpose. And without purpose, our life has no meaning.

Since so much of our identity comes from our work, it's important for our emotional, psychological, and spiritual well-being that we become more passionate about and engaged in what we do. Unfortunately, a common misconception is that one can feel passionate only about certain careers and that the others are just "jobs" to pay the bills. "It's easy for you to be passionate," a workshop participant once told me. "You have glamorous work. You get to travel all over the world teaching seminars and workshops. Some of us have to do the crummy jobs."

I have met people who are passionate about jobs that I would never want, like the plumber who came to help us with a flooded basement several summers ago. My husband had found him in the Yellow Pages. Then before he went off to teach his night school class, he told me someone would be coming around 7 p.m. When I went to the door, I found myself facing a man over six feet tall, with long, greasy hair and an unkempt beard. He was wearing a dirty white T-shirt with a pack of cigarettes rolled up in one sleeve, just like James Dean. His jeans were old, dirty, and tattered. His arms were covered with tattoos. He smiled and said, "Hi, I'm Jack. I understand you've got a problem with yer pipes." And that's when I noticed some of his teeth were missing. "Is this guy for real?" I thought. But there was something genuine about him.

"Follow me," I said. As soon as I got him to the flooded basement, his mastery began to show. He tried several things, all the while trying to isolate the problem. He seemed driven, working like a demon. I watched, impressed. My kids watched, fascinated.

Finally he stood up. "I've got to get my snake out of the truck. If that thing won't do it, ma'am, you probably have a bigger problem than I can solve. But my snake usually gets them all." With that, he rushed up the stairs.

I followed him, and that's when I noticed he had a woman passenger in his pickup. He brought the tool into the house, and when I asked him about his companion, he replied, "Oh, that's my girlfriend. I just picked her up from work." Apparently, coming over to fix our drain was more pressing than taking her home first.

Back downstairs we went, Jack, the snake, both my toddlers, and me. Once more we watched with fascination. After the steel snake had been fed into the drain and retrieved, it was still plugged. Then the plumber did something that made me want to throw up. He stuck his arm—right up to his armpit—into the drain and started feeling around. Then he pulled out a massive clump of stuff and looked up at me with satisfaction. "Ma'am, your problem is roots!" he announced with glee. His voice sounded like I had just won a million dollars.

To this day, I remain impressed by Jack's enthusiasm, energy, drive, and expertise. In short, the man was passionate about clogged pipes. Now, I wouldn't want to be sticking my arms into people's drains, but you could tell that Jack was born for this type of work. He took pride in it. He loved his work. The point is you can be passionate about anything. Whether or not others think it's disgusting or mundane or tedious doesn't matter. What matters is the attitude you bring to your work.

My father is retired now, but he's passionate about motors. His eyes widen when someone brings him a sick motor to be fixed. He loves the challenge of taking it apart and finding the problem. He can work on his tractor or truck for hours, often forgetting to eat or go home.

My mother's passion is her fruit farm and garden. The last time she was in Italy, when she buried her father, she brought back a tiny walnut seedling from her parents' garden. That seedling grew to over seventy feet high and now produces forty bushels of walnuts a year. For her, that tree is sacred. It carries the Spirit of her father, and every time she discovers a new walnut seedling, she says it's one of the babies of the original tree.

This is *passion* as a verb. This is the passion you bring with you to work, to your relationships, to everyday life. Being passionate is having an attitude and an energy inside you. It's a filter through which you look at the world. It's like permanent sunshine for the soul. This kind of passion is in the eye of the beholder. It's not some magical ingredient intrinsic to the work itself. There are no passionate jobs, only passionate people. The source of passion is *you*. It's the attitude you bring to your work that brings passion to your experience.

Perhaps you're thinking there's no way you can become passionate about your current job. Maybe you're in the right field but working the wrong hours. Perhaps you love some parts of your job but not others. Maybe you love the people but hate the structure; maybe you love your boss but hate the ethics of the company you work for. You may have some fine-tuning to do, and that's okay. We each deserve to hear our song played on all eighty-eight keys. If you're playing your song on fewer keys right now, maybe it's time to reconnect to your purpose. Passion can take you there.

YOUR PASSION IS LINKED TO YOUR PURPOSE

I want to be used up when I die. . . . Life is no brief candle to me. It is a sort of splendid torch which I have got hold of for a moment, and I want to make it burn as brightly as possible before handing it on to future generations.

—GEORGE BERNARD SHAW

Passion as a noun means your connection with a *what*; a thing; a person, place, or activity that brings out the best in you. It is a sacred link to your innermost Self, your own life force. It is a connection to Spirit, God, or the Universal Energy. Your passions are what you love and your loves define you. Your passions, not your bank account, tell the world who you are. By connecting to your passion, you stay authentic and true to yourself. Passion teaches us how to live.

For Barbara Braham, author of *Finding Your Purpose*, the words "passion" and "purpose" are synonymous. In fact, she says, when we dissect *passion* we find three words: *pass, I,* and *on*.[7] Passion, therefore, is about passing something of yourself on to the world. It's your legacy. It's your way of making a difference, your unique calling, your opportunity to bless the world with your gifts.

We are more than what we do to earn a living. The truth is that for some of us, what we do at our job doesn't come close to describing who we are. For some of us, it's only part of the story. Say you study the movement of planets or the mating habits of gorillas, or you spend most of your day changing wheels on trucks, cooking hamburgers, writing reports, making sales calls, building roads, or fixing pipes. Is that all you are? It may be your job, but it's not your purpose. Or it may be both your job and your purpose. How do you know?

Purpose has to do with meaning, and meaning is connected to passion. One of my favorite stories is about three bricklayers who are looking for work. During a job interview, the prospective employer asks each of them to describe what they did in their last job. The first bricklayer pipes up and says that he laid bricks. "That's what I did all day. I took bricks and mortar and put them together." Then the interviewer turns to the second bricklayer and asks him the same question. He says, "I built walls. I travelled to wherever they needed me to build walls." Finally, the interviewer turns to bricklayer number three. "Tell me, what did you do in your last job?" This bricklayer smiles as he pauses a moment to reflect. Then he leans in, eyes aglow, and says, "I built a cathedral."

If your work is your calling, if it's really what you were meant to do—your purpose—then you are building cathedrals every day, regardless of what type of work it is. Your ability to connect to the big picture is what nurtures not only meaning but also pride in what you do. Can you see the cathedral you're building, or do you feel at the end of the day that all you've done is laid bricks or built walls? Some leaders are helping their staff connect to the big picture by sharing the values and mission statement of the company. Still, finding meaning and purpose at work is your responsibility.

For those of you who may not know the differences between purpose, mission, and destiny, suffice it to say that passion is an ingredient of all of them. Our passions define us and point to our destiny. They also give us a reason to move our feet. A passionate embrace of your passions will fuel action. Passion doesn't come from the head; it comes from your heart. You feel it when you're not in the right job. You feel it when you're with the

wrong person. You feel it when you've betrayed your soul. It's time we paid attention to those feelings.

GETTING IN TOUCH WITH YOUR PASSIONS

I say follow your bliss and don't be afraid, and doors will open where you didn't know they were going to be.
—JOSEPH CAMPBELL

Okay, so you're convinced you want to live life with more passion. But how can one take off the mask of indifference? You might ask, "I want to connect to my passions, but how do I do it?" Here are five questions that will help you access your passions:

1. WHAT ARE YOUR LOVES?

Exploring what you are passionate about will help clarify who you are. In the nineteenth century, the German philosopher Friedrich Nietzsche said, "Your true being does not lie hidden deep inside you, but incalculably high above you. The question to ask yourself, looking back on your life, is 'What have I really loved?'"

Well, what do you love? What makes your heart sing? Follow your bliss, says Joseph Campbell. What is your bliss? When are you truly happy? Try different things until you discover what you love—and then go for it with all your heart. Don't hold back. What activity makes you feel excited and passionate? What makes the time fly when you're doing it?

Take out your journal and draw a heart in the center of the page. Inside the heart, write "My Passions." Then draw lines emanating from the heart like bicycle spokes. On these lines write your passions, your loves. Ask yourself, "What makes me happy? What makes me excited? Enthusiastic? What makes my Spirit soar?"

Your choices may be tangible things such as Italian food, palm trees, chocolate, your kids or your cat. Or they can be non-tangibles like rainy days, justice, beautiful sunsets, ideas, Sunday mornings. As you write, keep asking yourself, "What do I love? What do I care about? What's my bliss?" You'll have begun the journey to your passions. The truth is, once you commit to your passions, doors will open. It's one of those laws of life: Do what you love and the money will follow. Follow your bliss and the doors will open. Take the step and the bridge will be there.

2. WHAT ARE YOUR GUT FEELINGS?

Gut feelings have saved lives, discovered cures, and made people rich. They might come as a hunch, a flash, a deep knowing. The problem is that so many of us tune out our intuition in favor of something more logical or rational. But feelings are sacred. They are your barometer for what's really important. Go inward and listen. Keep a journal. Make friends with your feelings. Gut feelings are tugs on your heartstrings. They may arrive as an intuition, a hunch, a feeling that you know something, but you don't know how you know. Gut feelings come from the deepest part of you. You must learn to listen to them, pay attention, and learn from them.

It's not enough for people to know what to do to take the step—they must feel it in their gut. Feelings compel us to make fools of ourselves in love. Feelings are the inspiration that gives us the power to take risks, all kinds of risks. Feelings force us to take action. Knowledge is weak in comparison. Think about all the things that you already know you should be doing, like eating less junk food, exercising more, getting more sleep, spending more time with the kids. We all know by now that smoking is bad for our health, but that knowledge alone is not enough to make us take action. Rarely does knowledge alone motivate us to make the types of changes that will move our lives forward.

3. WHEN ARE YOU ENTHUSIASTIC?

Ralph Waldo Emerson once said that nothing great was ever achieved without enthusiasm. So, what is enthusiasm? As we learned in chapter 2, the root of enthusiasm is the Greek *entheos*, which means "filled with God" or "God within." Enthusiasm comes from your well of passion deep inside. It is holy. When you feel this way, your soul is speaking; you feel endless energy and exhilaration. Studies show that enthusiastic people have stronger immune systems because they're high on life. When you find yourself enthusing about something, pay attention! Your purpose is close by.

Bill Gates, the co-founder of Microsoft, is famous for saying "What I do best is share my enthusiasm." If you're enthusiastic about something, chances are your energy is contagious. You get people on board. You motivate a team, a community, a company. Management schools are trying to teach enthusiasm to our future leaders. The world needs more enthusiasm, because where enthusiasm lives, passion does, too.

4. WHAT INSPIRES YOU?

We have been trained to death. We have enough skills to solve all the world's problems, but what we lack is inspiration. When we're inspired, we take action. To get to our passions, we need to plug into our inspiration. The word "inspiration" is derived from the Latin verb *inspirare*, which means "to breathe into." The *Oxford English Dictionary* says that inspiration is "divine influence, especially that which is thought to prompt poets and that under which books of Scripture are held to have been written."

Sometimes when I'm in front of an audience I'll amaze myself by saying things that I never planned or that I didn't think I even knew. Then later someone will tell me how significant that story or example or metaphor was for them. When we're doing our life's work, it takes little effort, because we're visited by the muse of inspiration. Spirit is within us. Canadian singer/songwriter Loreena McKennitt called one of her recordings *The Visit* because, as she explains in the album notes, "the creative impulse is a visit . . . a thing of grace, mysterious. You don't know when it'll drop in."

When you are visited by this muse, you are blessed with creative genius. Creativity fertilizes the soul. Work is too often repetitive, boring, and meaningless, whereas humans are born to create. When our creative Spirit is restrained, it rebels. The individual Spirit yearns to be awakened and released. By its very nature, inspiration is transforming—its gifts are Spirit, "aliveness," and passion.

Like passion, inspiration can ignite action. I know this from personal experience. I can accomplish more in one hour when I'm inspired than in two weeks when I'm not. Simply put, when we're inspired, we take action. When we're not, we procrastinate. As a speaker, this is what I specialize in—inspiring people to take action. I tell stories and anecdotes. I share personal experiences. I get people involved, moving, laughing, thinking, and feeling. I bring a lot of energy to the front of the room, and the result is everyone leaves inspired. They think they've come to hear content, but the truth is that most people know what to do, they just don't do what they know. The missing ingredient is inspiration.

We're living in an Inspiration Economy. The coaching industry, which has exploded in the past few years, is a direct response to our need for inspiration. If we can't do it for ourselves, then we need a champion, someone encouraging us across the bridge, someone who believes in our greatness. When the heart is inspired, there are no limits. Desire is fueled, and change is possible.

So what if you can't afford your own personal coach? Does that mean that your well of inspiration is dry? In your journal, make a list of what inspires you. Then ask yourself, "What can I do today to inspire my heart and take one step towards my bridge?" For example, I knew I wanted to write this book, but attempting it all at once seemed overwhelming, especially when I was working and balancing my family responsibilities. But each time I felt my heart overflowing with inspiration, I would take out my journal and write down what I was feeling, sometimes only one or two ideas. Inspiration would come after seeing a great movie or reading stories of courage and faith;

after greeting the sunrise on a beach or hearing a beautiful piece of music; after a rich conversation with friends; or after delivering a really great seminar. I never waste inspiration. You might think that single ideas don't amount to much in themselves, but for me those single ideas eventually turned into the book you're now reading.

5. WHAT SYNCHRONICITIES HAVE YOU EXPERIENCED?

The term "synchronicity" was coined by psychologist Carl Jung to connote not just any coincidence, but meaningful coincidence. I first became aware of the magic of synchronicity after reading Milan Kundera's beautiful novel *The Unbearable Lightness of Being*. Kundera spends considerable time describing the meaningful coincidences that brought the two main characters, Tomas and Teresa, together. Kundera had his own word for these synchronistic events—he called them *fortuities*.

I believe that synchronicities can point you towards your passions or your higher purpose, like the book that you hear about but neglect to read, only to have it pop up everywhere you go. At the library, it falls off the shelf in front of you. You stop to have lunch with a friend, and the person next to you is reading it. You arrive home, and it's on your desk. Perhaps the Universe is sending you a message.

Synchronicities mark significant points of transition in our lives and point us in the direction of our purpose. We need to trust the hidden messages in synchronicities and pay attention to them when they happen. We tend to meet the "right" person, read the right book, hear the right song, or go to the right workshop when we're open to our spiritual journey and authentic calling. These synchronicities happen all the time to people tuned in to that higher frequency. Sometimes at my workshops people will say to me, "You know, I wasn't registered for this workshop. But then my friend got sick and I took her place. But now I realize that I *was* supposed to be here today, not my friend." For some people, it's the timing that is synchronistic. Spirit is always leading us by the hand.

Synchronicities also happen when you've listened to your heart and acted on an intuition. I was writing about the emperor penguins of Antarctica in order to illustrate to some clients the importance of teamwork and getting along. My memory of the details was vague, but I had been touched deeply by their story, which I had seen on educational TV years before. I was writing the story from the bits and pieces that I could remember. On one particular day I spoke to many people on the telephone, but only when I was talking to my friend John did a voice inside say, "Tell him about your penguin story." So I did. I shared with him how frustrated I was at not having time to track down more information on these amazing creatures.

That night when John went home he checked his mailbox and found that his *National Geographic* magazine had arrived that day. On the cover was a picture of emperor penguins—that month's feature story! He was stunned and so was I, but that's the power of the divine Mystery working in our lives.

The most amazing synchronicity that I've ever experienced has to do with my daughter's name. The summer after my first year of university, I took a job at the Calgary Stampede. I met many celebrities and media people that summer, and one of them was a journalist from Scandinavia. She was beautiful and smart, and I felt an immediate connection with her. Her name was Kajsa—pronounced kah-ee-suh. I had never heard the name before, but I loved it. I made a mental note that, should I ever have a daughter, that's what I would name her.

Later that fall, I met the man I was to marry. He was a mathematics major and an avid chess player. He was the only person I knew who owned a chess library, with hundreds of books on the subject. Chess was his passion, and he traveled to tournaments all over North America. Needless to say, he took the game very seriously.

Several years into our relationship—actually, while we were making wedding plans—I brought up the subject of kids' names. "I don't have a boy's name picked out,' I said, "but should we ever have a girl, I already have a name that I like."

"Oh?" he inquired. "What name is that?"

"Kajsa," I said.

I'll never forget the surprised look on his face. "Grace, Kajsa is the goddess of chess!"

That was in May 1982. Exactly ten years later, we were blessed with a baby girl. Of course, we named her Kajsa. And like her dad, she loves mathematics and chess. She's participated in a few chess tournaments already, and when she meets new opponents, especially boys, she'll let them know ever so gently that she was named after the goddess of chess.

Synchronicities—sacred coincidences—sometimes come to us like Delphic oracles telling us what to do next. They are messengers. They stand up and hit us on the head. Synchronicities are part of the language of people in love. Lovers yearn to be together all the time, but when they can't be, synchronicities are there to fill the void. For example, you meet a stranger at the bank and quite by accident find out his birthday. It's the same day as your beloved's. You're out driving and the numbers on the license plate of the car in front of you add up to her age. The restaurant you choose for lunch that day is featuring his favorite wine, and so on. Psychiatrist and past-life expert Brian Weiss says, "It is extremely important to pay attention to the coincidences, the synchronicities, and the déjà vu experiences in our lives, because they often represent the convergence of our spiritual plan and the actual path we are traveling during our lifetime."[8]

Synchronicities bring meaning to our lives. They remind us that there is a Mystery at work that we may not always understand but, if we pay attention, it can lead us to greater purpose. "Synchronicities, magical openings, omens, personalized revelations, oracles delivered by passing strangers . . . what do they prove?" asks Sam Keen in *The Passionate Life*. "That the world is more like a love affair than a battlefield."

Yes, indeed.

KEEPING PASSION ALIVE IN YOUR EVERYDAY LIFE

**We need to live each moment wholeheartedly,
with all our senses—finding pleasure in the fragrance of
a backyard garden, the crayoned picture of a six-year-old,
the enchanting beauty of a rainbow.**

—BARBARA BARTOCCI

The next time you go to a party, wait until you're asked the inevitable question, "What do you do?" Then break the mold and reply, "I'll tell you what I'm passionate about instead." Don't ask people what they do, because that may not define who they are. Ask them instead, "What are your passions? What do you love? What turns you on?" It's a risk, I know. But go for it—there is genius in boldness. If they give you weird looks, blame it on me.

Sarah Ban Breathnach, in her book *Something More*, talks a great deal about passion. She says that asking to be delivered to our passion is the only thing worth praying for. In fact, passion is so important to her that she had stenciled on her white bedroom walls—in gold letters, no less—the following definition, which she found on the back of a Passion Tazo tea bag: "True passion is intoxicating and invigorating, soothing and sensuous, magical and mystical. I just thought you should know what you're in for."[10]

Imagine yourself waking up to those words every morning. Do you think they would set the tone for your day? What is your definition of passion? How can you keep passion alive in your everyday life?

1. DECORATE YOUR PASSIONS

At my previous home, I did something I had never done before. I went crazy with the paintbrush. One night—actually, in the wee hours of the morning, while everyone was sleeping except Michelangelo wannabes like me—I painted several palm trees on the walls of my bathroom. I have always loved the shape of palm trees; as a child I sketched them endlessly. When I was done, I painted a huge heart with the infinity symbol above it to greet my husband in the morning. For seven years, those palm trees and heart greeted me each morning, and they gave me such a thrill. They were a testament to my passion.

In my office, instead of using a traditional fabric for the valance over my window, I opted for mauve wisteria flowers made of silk. They hang like clumps of ripe grapes, and they're delightful. Who says I can't use them as a valance? I'm sure some decorating professional would say I've done it all wrong, but I don't care. When you walk into my office, you can get a sense of the person I am. More importantly, when I'm there, I know who I am. Decorate your passions! Look around you.

What have you secretly wanted to do, but feared was not kosher decorating practice? Do it!

My friend Owen has motivational quotations all over his bathroom walls. They are written in a variety of fonts, weights, and colors, and each quotation is set at a different angle. The effect is a stunning inspirational menu for his bathroom guests. To decorate her basement, one of my clients had her children dip their hands into different colors of paint and make imprints on the whitewashed walls. The result is a border of handprints that will forever remind her of her precious ones after they have grown up and moved away. The point is that there are countless ways to express yourself and to decorate your passion. Be creative.

2. CREATE A SANCTUARY

I have always loved the colors of tropical beaches. That is where I feel my "bliss." Maybe it's because I was born near the Mediterranean, or maybe it's because I lived on a tropical island in a past life; I don't know. Throughout my travels, I've always been searching for the perfect beach. I found it—in Australia— and now I can see it on the walls of my office every day. I have a huge mural of the Whitsunday Islands near the Great Barrier Reef, the place I was visiting and, incidentally, where my first-born was conceived. (Another connection to passion!) Turquoise shades of water, palm trees, mountains, and white sand beaches greet me every morning as I walk into my office. More than any other room in the house, my office is my sanctuary.

Your environment is important. Surround yourself with what you love. I need nature. I need trees and many different shades of green. We moved to our current home because of the half-acre garden, the ravine behind the property, and the path to the lake. There are red cardinals, blue jays, and squirrels entertaining me daily. Yesterday, a hawk flew into my garden. He was huge and paused briefly before flying north towards the lake. It was a blessed moment.

My office contains so much of what I am passionate about: stacks and stacks of books and magazines; unique picture frames that hold photographs of the people I love most; candles; rocks and shells from the different places I've visited; and lots of angels. I get a lot of angels as gifts, and over the years I've built up quite a collection. More than anything, these angels are a reminder of the energy and love I put out into the world. Over the fireplace, I have a huge canvas of painted tulips (my favorite flowers) that are doing their own passionate dance. And, of course, I have many paintings, pictures, and cards, which my children have lovingly made for me over the years. When I look around in my sanctuary, I am reminded of how much I'm loved.

Which room in your home or office is your sanctuary? Which room could become one? Use colors that speak to you. Give in to that creative impulse that comes from your deepest core. Cover the beige walls with passion—your passion! Be outrageous. Let your authentic Self come out. Create a sanctuary.

3. LET YOUR SENSES TAKE IN THE WORLD

Give your senses a feast. Treat them to a sunrise, an elaborate meal, a symphony, silk sheets, or a fragrant garden. There is so much to see, hear, taste, smell, and experience. Our senses are a vehicle that allows us to experience our world with more passion and joy.

When was the last time you caught a sunset? A sunset is the promise of another day, but it's also the sun's way of making a splashy exit. It paints extravagant mauves and pinks across the sky, and it leaves an imprint on our souls. Do you remember your most beautiful sunset? In her book *A Natural History of the Senses*, Diane Ackerman tells us how, no matter what is going on at the office, she honors her ritual of watching the sunset from the picture window in her living room. She writes, "Each night the sunset surged with purple pampas-grass plumes and shot fuchsia rockets into the pink sky, then deepened through folded layers of peacock green to all the blues of India and a black across which clouds sometimes churned like alabaster dolls. The visual opium of the sunset was what I craved . . ."[11] That is one passionate sunset and one passionate woman!

My friend Catherine and I are moon goddesses—we love the moon. In 1999, Earth experienced two blue moons, one in January and one in March. A blue moon is the second full moon in less than a month. They are not really that rare, since they happen every couple of years, but two blue moons in one year *is* rare (the last one happened in 1961).

We weren't going to let the opportunity pass without a celebration. My fellow moon goddess and I got permission to eat outside on the balcony of a beautiful restaurant overlooking Lake Ontario so we could see the blue moon rising over the lake. It was March and not all that warm, but there we were, bundled up in our coats, enjoying our meal, our wine, and a perfect view of the full moon rising over the moonlit water. It was simply breathtaking.

My friend Addie loves to cook. She doesn't just cook; she makes love to food. Addie is to food as Juliette Binoche was to chocolate in the movie *Chocolat*. She said to me the other night, "Don't you hate it when you go to lunch with someone and they say, 'Oh, I'll just have a salad'? God, when there are so many wonderful things to eat!" Addie loves to feed her friends. When we go to her house, the divine smells from her kitchen beckon us from the driveway. She's always got some new recipe for us to try. Visiting her kitchen is like taking your taste buds on an adventure. Can you cook with abandon, or do you cook within the lines? Can you take your taste buds on an adventure? Do you experiment? Be passionate—spice up your life! Choose a new vegetable, one you've never cooked before. Try an exotic fruit. Share a decadent dessert. Let the different tastes and textures make love to your palate.

As soon as I step into Lola's car, I'm engulfed in the high-octane vibrations of Latino music. She's bouncy and excited. *"Ciao, bella!* You're not going to believe the song I found. Listen to this!" Then she cranks it up—loud enough, I'm convinced, to wake the dead in Argentina—and we cruise down the road to a pounding beat. Outside, it's cold, gray, and windy, but in the car we might as well be in her native Puerto Rico. Lola appreciates music in a way that most people don't. At her house parties, she turns her living room into a dynamic disco, complete with lights, lasers, and smoke. She's always the DJ, and she always manages to get even the shy ones up and dancing. What music are you passionate about?

The point is there is so much to be passionate about. Feast your senses on the passionate universe. Experience the colors, tastes, sounds, and textures around you. Get intimate with life.

4. DEVELOP A GRATITUDE ATTITUDE

The more gratitude you teach your heart, the more it will fill with passion. I was in Florida and really wanted to see dolphins in the wild. After several dolphin-watching expeditions, I was disappointed that none had showed up.

We were staying right on the beach near Fort Myers. Early each morning, while my family was still sleeping, I would sneak out with my music and my running shoes and go for a long run along the beach. On the last morning, to my delight, three dolphins showed up to say hello. They accompanied me on my run for nearly two miles, swimming close to shore beside me. Every now and then, they'd jump out of the water and do somersaults, squealing with delight like three little children. I couldn't believe my luck! Had they perhaps heard the calling of my heart? I stopped to soak it all in. The beautiful beach, inspirational music in my ears, and the happy dolphins beside me— it was almost too much for my heart to take. It was a blessed moment. Gratitude began spilling out of me, and I looked up at the sky and shouted, "Thank you, thank you, thank you!"

We were meant to be grateful for the privilege of being alive. The reward for our gratitude is a greater passion for life. Wake up every morning exhilarated and ready to take on the day. When you feel blessed by perfect moments, secretly look up and say thank you. What are your perfect moments, and do you give thanks for them?

EMBRACE YOUR PASSION

You can have anything you want if you want it passionately enough. You must want it with an inner exuberance that erupts through the skin and joins the energy that created the world.

—SHEILA GRAHAM

Those who live their lives from passion are filled with light— they are leading authentic lives. They're living the life they want, not one that has been handed down to them. They live their truth. Passionate people savor life. They teach us how to love. They teach us how to live.

Passion is far more than the white-hot obsession felt between two people, although it is that, too. It is the fire we feel in our hearts when perfect moments come together and we are free to express who we are. Keeping passion alive is about courage, the courage to be who you are, regardless of the consequences. Living with passion is about living on the edge—it's about pushing yourself to grow outside your comfort zone. By being true to your passion, you live authentically, truthfully, joyfully. Passion drives action. It will thrust you across your bridge towards that which is waiting to move your life forward. Squeeze the juice out of your life. Passion is your soul's duty. Don't apologize for your passion, and don't extinguish your fire for anyone.

4

Heal Your Past

BEGIN THE HEALING JOURNEY

You are caught by what you are running from.

—SAM KEEN

"Grace, he finally cried. It was all because of that movie. I never knew it would have such an impact on him!" Judy had been complaining to me about her husband's indifference and lack of passion for quite some time. Now she couldn't wait to tell me how the movie *My Life* had triggered Bill's healing journey.

The main character, played by Michael Keaton, has been diagnosed with terminal cancer and has only a few months to live. His wife, played by Nicole Kidman, is pregnant with their first child. He begins to record himself on video talking to his unborn baby, making a record of his life for the son he might not live to see. He desperately wants to be a father to this child, so he tells him about his heritage, where he was born and where he grew up. But when he gets to pictures and home movies of his childhood with his parents and brother, buried emotions—anger, disgust, shame, and hurt—begin to surface.

At his wife's insistence, the man sees a Chinese doctor who supposedly cured a friend's father of cancer. He is skeptical, but goes anyway. The doctor tells him he has a lot of anger and that the tumors will go away when he learns to forgive. As the doctor is performing a healing-energy massage on his chest, Keaton's character sees a white light and has a strange experience. Frightened, he bolts off the table and leaves. "What did the doctor say?" his wife wants to know. "He says I'm angry and that I have to forgive. Stupid quack! I'm not angry! Who do I have to forgive?" he yells.

This is the story of a man coming to terms with his bottled-up past, the feelings of hurt and anger that he felt as a child but never voiced. He finally does make peace with his parents and forgives them, but it is too late. Although he now has faith in alternative medicine, the tumors have spread to his brain. He spends his last days at home surrounded by his wife, his parents, and his brother, and that's when he makes peace with his family and with himself.

In one scene, the dying man's father gives him a shave. Obviously touched, the son slowly reaches up to touch his father's hand, pauses, and whispers, "I love you, Dad."

That's when it happened. Bill's lower lip began to quiver. He started crying softly at first, but then the dam broke. He sobbed as Judy had never seen him sob before. He collapsed on the floor with his head on her lap, and she held him tight. He cried; he moaned. The sounds that tore from his throat were primitive and full of anguish. His body shook with the force of the wails that came from deep within him. The tears kept coming and coming; sorrow swept over him like a blanket, engulfing them both.

Judy said later that it felt as though she were giving birth—to his tears, to his pain, to his healing journey. He kept quivering, shaking, one contraction after another, one moan after another, as she held on to him, whispering words of encouragement. When the trembling finally subsided, her chest and lap were completely soaked from his tears. Judy had been Bill's midwife, helping to usher in his tears.

Then Bill began to speak. "All I wanted was his touch, his love. I just wanted him to be my dad. But he ignored me. I was invisible. I was robbed! I hated him—and *I turned into him!*" With this realization, his body went into spasms, vibrating with energy fueled by his disbelief and shock. He howled in agony.

And then it was as though an arrow had pierced his heart. His pain climaxed, and he was left limp and wasted. However, the wound of Bill's realization went deeper and deeper, until he lay curled up on the floor. Judy lay on the carpet with him, soothing him and loving him. He was soaked and spent, and so was she. As she lay there, stroking Bill's hair, she heard a sudden patter of raindrops outside. There was no thunder or lightning—just a gentle, cleansing rain. She opened a window and let the spray of that cleansing rain wash over Bill's face. Her husband had lost his father nearly twenty years earlier, but only now was he finally grieving his death and, more importantly, the relationship he never had with him. Bill had finally reached a point where he could begin to heal the past.

In this chapter, I will tell you about some ideas and practices that I have used to heal myself and people who have come to me with the same need. Ultimately, the best advice I can give you is to follow your own heart. Trust your instincts. Try the approaches that speak to you. Some people advocate leaving the past alone, but I believe that healing and learning from our past are necessary to remove the obstacles to faith in who we are and what we can achieve.

Buddhists use a phrase that means "no escape." Sometimes when life becomes unbearable, we want to run away—so we leave our families, move to a different city, change jobs, remarry, and start over again. And then, sooner or later, we find ourselves dealing with the very issues and people and problems we thought we'd left behind. "No escape" means that what we run from follows us. What we don't heal will always be with us.

HEAL THE INNER FAULT LINES

Running away from suffering intensifies it; denying suffering intensifies it; wallowing in suffering intensifies it; blaming our suffering on others intensifies it. Anesthetizing it will work for only so long. And emotional shutdown is ultimately destructive to mind and body.

—GABRIELE RICO

Most people at first glance seem happy and together. They're competent in at least some areas of their lives. They've learned how to play the game, they juggle their many roles and responsibilities, and most of the time they appear to keep it all under control. But what the outside world doesn't see is the fault lines on the inside, which are susceptible to pressure.

Earthquakes occur along fault lines. Pressure builds beneath the earth's crust until the tectonic plates "slip" along a fault line and an earthquake results. In human terms, once sufficient stress has built up over time, the fault line will lead to a dramatic life event. The event could be, for example, a heart attack, diagnosis of a disease (the disease develops over time, of course, but its detection can be a shock), or the breakup of a marriage. By healing the fault line, however, we can pre-empt the dramatic event. If there is no fault line, no earthquake can happen.

Like Earth, we are riddled with internal fault lines. Unlike Earth, we have the potential to heal our fault lines one by one. What are these fault lines? They could be an abusive past, spiritual emptiness, feeling unwanted or unloved, clogged emotions, low self-esteem, anxiety, depression, or loneliness.

In her book *Pain and Possibility*, Gabriele Rico talks about the death of her mother in a bombing raid when Rico was only seven years old. For many years, she imagined there was a long, jagged crack across her heart, and she wondered if she would ever heal from it. As an adult Rico concludes, "We're all damaged somehow, somewhere—the real issue is not whether, but how, we learn to deal with our damage."[1]

When his parents divorced, my client Marco was only ten years old. For reasons that are still unclear to him, he was sent to live with relatives in Spain. They were mean to him. Both his father and mother remarried in his native Nicaragua, but they never sent for him. He grew up feeling abandoned and unloved.

It's always when we're at the threshold of change that the question of healing our past emerges. "Cross that bridge," the nasty demons warn you, "but deal with us."

"No, not today," you reply. "I can't face you today." So you turn back. But Spirit grows impatient. It pushes you to take that step towards your destiny. Somewhere deep within you, you hear the voice saying, "It's time." As you look inside, you see a tarnished mirror reflecting back all the tears you've never cried, the hurts that never healed—an infinite well of sadness. No Band-Aids will work. The wounds are still fresh, even now, after so many years. They've been waiting for you, waiting for the day when you have the courage to face them and heal them. Your soul has a special destiny. It wants to fly, but it can't fly if the emotional wounds of the past are not healed.

We must make friends with our past and take responsibility for it if we are to heal and reclaim our power. We all have "stuff" from our childhood locked in that Pandora's box deep inside us, stuff that needs healing. But most of us are unaware of it.

The healing journey is deeply personal, and there are many paths one can take. Every experience we bring into our lives becomes an opportunity to grow our souls and heal the past. Those experiences are the steppingstones on which we build our lives. They are the ladders to healing and fulfilling our mission here on earth. But while the paths are as varied as the individuals, there is a common destination. People want rich, meaningful lives filled with deep spiritual connections and loving relationships.

Meaningful healing takes place when there is a change of heart, expansion of consciousness, letting go, forgiveness, release of emotion, acceptance of something previously denied, or reconnection. Healing the past can happen on many levels. It is not only a cure of the body, but a cure of the Spirit as well.

DO YOU HAVE A SHADOW?

Everyone is a moon, and has a dark side which he never shows to anybody.
—MARK TWAIN

Everyone has a shadow. It is the sum of the aspects of your Self that you deny, repress, or disown. It's those things that made us feel shame or brought us punishment when we were children. We would rather hide that part of us in the closet or sweep it under the rug. But to be truly authentic and to reclaim our wholeness, we have to allow the qualities in ourselves that we love and accept to coexist with the parts of ourselves that we hate and disown.

Poet Robert Bly says the shadow is "the long bag we drag behind us." It is filled with character traits, emotions, and talents that were unaccepted by our family and friends. Bly believes we spend the first twenty years of our lives filling up our bags, and the rest of our lives trying to empty them.

When we are moving strongly towards abundance and positive thinking, why would we want to bother with the shadow? Why would we want to illuminate the monsters in the darkness? Why would we want to open that Pandora's box? The reason is this: Who you are is a totality. Over the years you have played one side more than the other, and you have lost your balance. In an effort to regain equilibrium, you have attracted into your life people and experiences that reflect the aspects of yourself you've disowned.

Here's an example. Susan is kind, giving, and accommodating. But she has disowned her anger—the part of herself that would stand up for her rights, that would say no, that would have the courage to roar like a lion if necessary. Consequently, Susan keeps attracting selfish and aggressive people who take advantage of her.

When we bring our wholeness to a relationship, we attract others who are whole and balanced. We can see the sun because we have experienced the darkness. We know peace because we've experienced war. We know love because we've felt the fear. When we embrace all that we are, we're healing all that we pushed aside in the past.

"A soulful life is never without shadow," says Thomas Moore in his book *Care of the Soul*. In fact, "some of the soul's power comes from its shadow qualities."[2] Embracing our shadows allows us to live authentically and purposefully. When we have the courage to say yes to all our moods, emotions, and qualities, then we've entered the realm of possibility. We have a wide range of options from which to create our lives. When we can express the totality of who we are and live from our depths—passionately, intensely, soulfully, and without fear— then we come into the power that is our birthright. We become spiritual warriors, ready to take action and move our lives and our communities forward.

OPEN THE DOORS IN YOUR CASTLE

Within every human being there are gods and goddesses in embryo with only one desire. They want to be born.
—DEEPAK CHOPRA

"When you understand that you contain everything you see in others, your entire world will alter," says Debbie Ford in her book *The Dark Side of the Light Chasers*. "The key is to understand that there is nothing we can see or perceive that we are not."[3] What she is suggesting is a holistic model of the Universe. It teaches that each of us is a microcosm of the macro, that we contain every aspect of the Universe. We are all that we see, all that we judge, all that we admire. Just imagine what that would be like—to realize that within you is every quality, every emotion, every attitude, every state of being, and that you can choose to call forth whatever you wish from within yourself. What a concept!

I like psychologist John Welwood's analogy of the castle to illustrate the world within us. Imagine being a beautiful castle with thousands of exquisite rooms. Each room is beautiful in its own way, and each possesses a special gift. These rooms represent different aspects of your Self. As a child, you loved each room. In fact, you were altogether carefree and fearless, and regardless of what kind of room it was, you always found something that made it special. Your castle was full of light, love, and wonder.

Then one day someone arrived and told you that one of your rooms was ugly. They suggested you close it off and lock the door. Since you wanted their love and approval, you agreed. Then, more people arrived and started complaining. Everyone had his or her opinion about the rooms. To accommodate them, you shut the doors on more of the rooms in your castle. Eventually, it became a habit, and you closed rooms because you were afraid they were becoming ugly. Sometimes you compared your castle to others and decided that some of your rooms didn't measure up. Soon you found yourself living in just a few rooms.

You forgot that you lived in a castle with thousands of rooms. You stopped taking risks, stopped believing in your magnificence, stopped feeling joy.

RECLAIM YOUR WHOLENESS

We are not there until we can say "yea" to it all.

—JOSEPH CAMPBELL

The castle metaphor shows poignantly how we begin the cycle of disowning who we are. When we embark on our healing journey, we need to throw open the doors to all of the rooms in our castles. But how can we go into those rooms when we're afraid? How can we reclaim the things that make us uncomfortable or that we would rather not look at? You know—the rooms called "stupid" or "selfish" or "arrogant" or "lazy." Surely we are not really like that. If you're serious about changing the direction of your life and healing your past, you must go into each room and find the positive potential of each quality.

What do I mean by the positive potential? If stupidity is something you disown (your shadow self), ask yourself, "What is the positive potential of stupidity?" In other words, how do you need to view stupidity in order for you to reclaim your wholeness? For example, contrast these two ways of being:

- I do something stupid. My co-worker screams at me and calls me stupid. I feel bad, accept the label, and now think that I am stupid. I start working hard never to be stupid again. My motivation for love and acceptance is so great that I disown this part of myself. (This is a person who has closed off the "stupid" room of his castle.)
- I do something stupid, but I won't accept the label. I accept that I *did* something stupid, but not that I *am* stupid. I don't disown stupidity—I just allow myself the possibility that I will do stupid things sometimes because I'm human. In other words, I accept that there is a room in my castle called "stupid" and that sometimes, intentionally or not, I may visit.

One way to meet your shadow is to start off by finding the positive potential of your disowned selves. In other words, what else did you give up when you closed that room of your castle? How might it have put pressure on your fault lines?

In the space on page 122, write down six of your positive qualities, using words that best describe you and those qualities that you're proud of. Then in the second column, write down the opposite of each quality in the "positive" column. These opposites don't have to be an exact antonym according to the dictionary, just what you would say in your own words. So, for example, if you wrote down "loving" as one of your positive qualities, ask yourself what would be the opposite of loving. For some people it might be "callous," for others "cold," for others "mean." It's important to write down your own word. Be aware of any repeat words or patterns you see emerging. Column two represents your shadow. These are the rooms in your castle that you've closed off for whatever reason. One way we can open them up again is to tell ourselves that our shadow holds the key to our healing.

Positive Qualities	Shadow Self	Positive Potential (The Gift)
1 smart	stupid	
2 loving	cold	
3 fast	slow	
4		
5		
6		

Column 3 is where you become creative. Take the disowned quality and reinterpret it in a positive way that makes sense to you. For example, three of my positive qualities are that I'm smart, loving, and fast. For me the opposite of *smart* is *stupid*, the opposite of *loving* is *cold*, and the opposite of *fast* is *slow*. I have certainly disowned *stupid*; all my life I've generated esteem by being smart. Because I was the oldest child in my family, my parents depended on me to solve problems and be a role model for my brothers. Once I was able to give myself permission not to know it all, not to be the "consummate seminar leader" (as a friend once called me), to make mistakes and not have to educate the entire world, then I could see *stupid* in a positive way. When someone presents me with a problem, I don't have to jump to solve it. I can say I don't know and refer them elsewhere. Your positive potential gives you permission to embrace the opposite, so you can come into balance with yourself.

As for *cold*, I really disowned it. *Cold* was a room in my castle I'd shut down for good. My family, especially my mom's side, are all very loving. I was taught to show respect by hugging and kissing everyone who came to the house. I'm naturally warm and compassionate, so that wasn't hard for me. I greet all my friends with hugs, and sometimes my clients, too. After my workshops I usually have a long line of people waiting to hug me.

So what could possibly be the positive potential of *cold*? Well, I could learn to stop being judgmental about myself when I don't feel like chatting to a stranger on the plane or when I don't feel like being nice or friendly. I need to tell myself that I don't always have to be caring, nurturing, and compassionate with everyone. Sometimes I need to say no and take care of myself first. Sometimes I need to detach and restore my energy. I didn't used to be good at this, often giving too much and then later resenting it or feeling drained. But now I no longer disown *cold*.

I had disowned *slow*. Everything about me is fast. I think fast, make decisions fast, drive fast, and walk fast. Consequently, I used to get impatient frequently. I'm also a doer and can't stand indecision and inaction. So whom do I marry? A slow and thorough man. This is the Universe's way of balancing me. I love life and have this greed for living and experiencing everything I can. This is not a bad thing, but what did I need in order to become more whole and balance my energy? I needed to learn to just *be*. I've learned to meditate, do yoga, be still, and pray. I've learned not to beat myself up for just staring out the window and daydreaming. I no longer try to jam-pack my day. I've embraced my *slow*ness, and I'm a better person for it.

If you get stuck on the positive potential, ask yourself what gift your shadow has for you. What do you need to give yourself permission to be or do? How can you bring your life into greater balance? The positive potential of any disowned quality is an interpretation—there are no wrong answers. Think about it; talk about it. If it makes sense to you, that's all you need to meet your shadow. By allowing yourself to be what you have disowned, buried, or pushed aside, you are healing those parts of yourself that you don't yet love or accept. Open the doors in your castle and let the sun shine in. It's time to celebrate all that you are, to reclaim your wholeness. Carl Jung once said that he would rather be whole than good. What part of yourself have you sacrificed in order to be good? What masks have you assumed to please others? Know that the world needs *all* of you.

WRITE DOWN YOUR PAIN

Spilling your pain onto the page is healing; holding it in is as unfruitful as holding your breath. Letting go leads to life.
—GABRIELE RICO

Soon after giving birth to my first child, Jasper, I decided to take a creative writing class. During that class, we were encouraged to meditate on some aspect of our childhood and then to pick up our pens and start writing. The instructor was irreverent, funny, and intense. "Anything at all," she'd say. "Let the story bubble up. Just keep writing until I say stop." It was then that I became aware of some of my "stuff"—childhood stories, unexpressed emotions, memories that had slipped out of consciousness. They were rich and textured, and brought me face-to-face with my past.

*I am a little girl about seven years old, sitting on the outside steps
at the side door to my house. It's dark and cold. I'm crouched
down, hugging my knees to stay warm and rocking back and
forth. I'm alone. I'm waiting for daylight so I can go to school.
My father has already left for work. I'm too small to lock the door
myself, so he locks the door and leaves me outside. My mother is
in the hospital. She had my little baby brother a few weeks ago,
but now she's in the hospital again. When the sun comes out
and I see people walking, that's my cue to walk to school. I'm
not scared.*

In the back of my mind, I had always known this story, but I
was not aware that I had unexpressed emotions about it.
Reading it aloud to the class, I started to cry. I had found a
wound. Slowly other childhood stories and emotions began to
bubble up. It was time for me to deal with my stuff. My healing
journey started then and continues today. We don't always
understand why people do the things they do, but healing leads
you to greater intimacy and truth in your relationships. Because
my dad has always been fiercely independent, I know now that
it wouldn't have occurred to him to leave me at a neighbor's. I
was given responsibility at a young age. I am the person I am
today because of my parents' confidence in me.

Creative writing or journaling is one way of accessing
repressed feelings from the past. In my healing retreats with
women, I get them to bring three photographs of themselves as
children. I instruct them to write a letter to their inner child, tell
her what she would have liked to hear, the encouraging words
that were missing from her childhood. I'm always amazed at
the power of this exercise. Writing is a gateway to healing and
personal transformation and it is possible to explore pain
through language.

Do you keep a journal? Look at some childhood pictures. Close your eyes, take a deep breath, and visualize a memory from your past. Don't judge it; just go with it, whatever it is. Then pick up a pen and let the memory guide you. Write about it. Use writing as a vehicle for healing and self-discovery. Make connections, see the patterns, and reconnect with your memories. The act of writing loosens the pain encrusted on your emotional walls. It will help you unearth the disowned parts of your Self. It will help the stories of your past percolate up. It will throw open the doors in your castle.

LET YOUR STORIES OUT

Love me, love my story. Human intercourse is an intermingling of flesh and story.

—SAM KEEN

Our lives are stories, and by expressing our stories, we heal. That's why we seek out therapists, friends, and family members who will listen to them. We have all, at some time or another been wounded emotionally, psychologically, or physically. The stories that make up our lives comprise our identity, our history, our individuality. Stories are the language of the heart. They connect our human drama. We need to be heard. We need someone to bear witness to our lives. I feel blessed because people trust me with their stories. My husband teases me that I have "Compassionate Therapist" branded on my forehead. Why else would absolute strangers pour out their intimate stories to me in grocery checkout lines, on airplanes, and at my seminars (though it's more understandable at my seminars)? They've heard me speak, and they feel they know me, like the woman who wrote me the following letter.

Dear Grace:

I feel compelled to write to you. Last week when I heard you speak, I had been feeling an endless despair. Needless to say, I am feeling better. My whole marriage has been spent trying to conceive a baby. It didn't happen, and probably won't now, and I do not want to adopt. I am in turmoil, but in spite of it all, my heart still whistles a tune and I really do not want to leave this earth. It was comforting to hear your hopeful and empowering words. The paradox in all of this is that I feel as though I am going through labor to give birth to myself, and it hurts so much. I don't mean to be so self-centered. I just wanted to share my story with you.

Our stories tell people who we are. They reveal secrets, hopes, and dreams. They express our deepest longings. It's our stories that make us real. When we express them, we heal. What stories may be percolating up for you? Your stories are rich threads woven together to make the tapestry that is your life. Choose to remember the stories from your past. Share them. Do it tonight over dinner. Tell your beloved a story about your childhood. Tell your children; tell your staff; tell a friend. Or tell it to the white page that is waiting to help you heal.

HEALING SHIFTS

Hidden wounds have hidden agendas that hold us hostage to the past.
—PAUL FERRINI

I'm convinced that sometimes an "aha" moment, or what I like to call an SFI (Sudden Flash of Insight), can let you make a quantum leap of healing. I've had such moments in my life, and I've also shared the experience as other people "get it." Sometimes it occurs when I teach workshops or seminars; other times it happens when I'm coaching or counseling. I see it on their faces, in their eyes. Their posture shifts. Frowns relax and illumination appears. It's almost as though you can hear their souls say, "Ah, I see." Such moments are one of my biggest professional highs. When you suddenly see another way or a different perspective or a reason for something, it's like all the puzzle pieces finding their spots at once. Everything clicks and a shift takes place. These shifts are healing; they change our perception. They're like laser beams of awareness that burn their healing marks on our consciousness.

"Miss Cirocco, I'm wondering if you have a few moments to talk to me," asked Theresa, a relative of the person who had invited me to speak at a seminar. I looked at my watch. It was almost time to begin my presentation, but I sensed a real yearning and need, so I guided her to a quiet corner and said, "Sure, what can I do for you?"

"It's my life. It's coming apart. I don't know what to do . . . " and then she burst into tears.

Offering her a tissue, I asked, "What's the problem?"

"I've been married three years and I have a two-year-old son, but I don't know whether I can stay with my husband."

"Why? Is he hurting you?"

"Oh, no, he's kind and gentle and wonderful."

"Well, then, what's the problem?"

"He has this mental disease—he takes pills—he's manic-depressive."

"Does his disease get in the way? Does it hurt your relationship? Does he ever hurt you or the child?"

"No, it's not like that. He takes his medication and he's okay."

"Well, then, what's the problem?"

And finally, Theresa got to the root of her worries. "Everyone knew about his problem before we got married except me. Nobody told me."

Oh, now I understood. "So you're feeling betrayed, deceived, tricked?"

The tears streamed from her eyes. I could see the depth of pain she had been holding inside, and I hugged her.

"I can't talk to anyone about this. All my friends and family were in on it," she told me, as we continued to embrace.

"They must have felt this man was the right choice for you and that if you knew the truth you might have passed him up," I rationalized for her.

"Yes, that's what they say now, but I still should have known."

"So, what do you want to do about it?" I asked her.

"I don't know. I'm confused. I feel as if I've made another big mistake—this is my second marriage. Now I have a child with him, and I feel like I've really messed up my life. I can't sleep; I can't eat. No one understands. I don't know what to do."

I looked at the clock and saw that there was no time. Suddenly I got an inspiration. "Betrayal hurts a lot," I told her. "You have a right to feel hurt. Your family had their reasons, but it still doesn't make it right. You wanted to marry him with all the cards on the table. But now you're married and you have a son with him, and you tell me you love him. Let me ask you this: Had you known about his illness before your marriage, would you still have gone through with the wedding?"

By her reaction, I knew this was the question Theresa needed to hear. This was the question that would pierce her heart and give her the illumination and peace she so desired. She paused and her jaw dropped. It was a blessed moment. She looked deep into my eyes, and a tiny smile came to her lips.

"Yes," she said. "I would still have married him." And then

she let out a huge sigh of relief and asked incredulously, "Oh my God, how did you do that?"

"I didn't do it, you did!" I replied.

"Thank you, thank you, thank you," Theresa said, throwing herself into my arms. "I feel like I'm out of jail!"

When people heal, they are transformed. For the rest of the evening, Theresa was floating, interacting with others in a carefree, happy-go-lucky way. Her husband arrived after the workshop to pick her up, and she introduced me to him. I could see his gentleness immediately from the way he helped her with her coat, the way he looked at her. "She is blessed with a good man," I thought.

Sometimes forgiving or letting go of the past seems like it can take forever. And sometimes, as in Theresa's case, it can take five minutes—if the right question is asked. In the Arthurian legends, Sir Perceval loved asking questions, but by the time he became a brave knight of King Arthur's Round Table, he had been convinced to curb his questioning. By listening to others, he lost touch with his own authentic voice. One night while at the Grail Castle, Perceval dines with the wounded Fisher King. As the king and the knight converse, a procession passes before them carrying the fabulous Holy Grail. Perceval is being tested. If he asks the right question—"Whom does the Grail serve?"— the Fisher King will be healed and the surrounding wasteland will be restored to a paradise. He fails and, as a punishment, is placed under a spell. Perceval spends five years wandering alone in the wasteland, not knowing who he is or how to cure his malaise. One day, exhausted and spent, he stops to ask a stranger, "What day is it today?" At that moment, the spell is broken. Apparently, the act of asking a question did it. Perceval is healed and free to rejoin the rest of the knights of the Round Table.

Like Perceval, I think we're all suffering under a similar spell. We seem to be drifting in our own personal wastelands without a compass and without our souls. Healing ourselves and our planet will come when we learn to ask the right questions. Beware of the army of experts out there that's ready to tell you what's wrong with you and to prescribe a medley of solutions. Sometimes all you need to do in order to heal is to ask the right question. What question do you need to be asking? What question can, as in Theresa's case, help you heal your heavy heart?

DARK NIGHTS OF THE SOUL

The dark night of the soul comes just before revelation.
—JOSEPH CAMPBELL

Healing the past brings us face-to-face with our "dark night of the soul." In the sixteenth century, the Spanish mystic St. John of the Cross coined this phrase to designate the part of our journey in which we lose our inner compass and fall victim to fear, loneliness, depression, and pain. The dark night of the soul can be our worst nightmare, but it also can be a rich time for learning and spiritual growth.

Spiritual growth means growing our souls, and growing our souls means becoming better at being human beings. But when we're in the throes of the dark night of the soul, we feel hopeless. This is the valley that Theresa was living in before her "shift" in thinking. This is the wasteland that Perceval was sent to during the five-year spell. Our minds start playing tricks on us, and we fall deeper and deeper into a chasm of despair. We ask, "How can it possibly be a positive experience?"

I have had clients who I knew were not ready to heal, because they hadn't experienced their dark night of the soul. Therapists call this "hitting rock-bottom"—you can't come up, until you've gone all the way down. You can't heal your pain, until you've had the courage to embrace all of its raw intensity. Mystics and sages of the past teach us that pain brings us closer to God, that it can fuel the fire of purification, taking us further along in our spiritual journey. For them suffering intensifies the search for what is most sacred. Even generations ago, pain was not something to be avoided; it was simply a part of life. And the more pain you endured, the more respect people paid you. The thinking went that the more suffering one did, the more one was blessed with wisdom.

When I was twenty and away at university, I got a telephone call that rocked my world. "Dad has been in a car accident," the voice said. "He's hurt pretty badly. The doctors say there's a fifty-fifty chance he won't make it. Please come home right away. Tony and I need you." The voice belonged to my teenage brother, John. The accident had happened while my mother was in Europe visiting her parents. As I boarded the train for the five-hour journey home, my heart was full of terror. So many questions came to mind. What if he died? What if Mom couldn't make it home on time? How were my brothers, John and Tony, coping? Why did Mom have to go away? How was I going to do it without her?

My mind was racing while the train seemed to crawl from one town to another. I was feeling overwhelmed, alone, and frightened. "Hurry up, train, I want to see my daddy alive," I sobbed. I stared out the window, trying really hard not to let the other passengers hear me crying. Then out of nowhere a woman sat down next to me. We hadn't made a stop to pick up new passengers—she had just been walking up the aisle and had decided to sit next to me. She saw my tears and invited me to share my suffering.

"Some day, Grace," she said, with love in her eyes, "this experience will feed your art." They were strange words, but they were exactly what my soul needed to hear. Her words had the same effect on me as the question I posed to Theresa. Sometimes God sends us angels when we most need them. I know she was sent to comfort me in my moment of darkness, just as I was sent to Theresa.

I interpreted her statement to mean that my pain would transform itself to make me a stronger, wiser Grace. I would grow, and the strength and wisdom would some day translate into my "art." In *The Heart Aroused*, American poet David Whyte alludes to a similar concept when he says, "It is the embrace of failure and grief, harrowing as these are, that forms the vessel for the joyous votive flame of creativity."[4] Many of his own poems were created that way.

Carl Jung spoke of an archetype called the "wounded healer." Perhaps each wound we suffer and eventually heal from has the potential to grow us as humans so that we can, with time, participate in the healing of our world. I know that my suffering has made me a better counselor, workshop facilitator, mother, and friend. And yet sometimes I don't think I've suffered at all. I think about the unbearable cruelties and torture that are going on right now on this planet, and I weep. I watch movies, read books, and hear stories of personal hardship, and I grieve along with them. It seems that some people are cursed with more than their share. That seems wrong.

But a different point of view might suggest that those sufferers are the chosen, the blessed. They have had an opportunity to heal and grow their souls. They are the enlightened ones, further along in their journey. Medical doctor and psychologist Joan Borysenko says in her book *Fire in the Soul: A New Psychology of Spiritual Optimism* that ". . . even the most painful and seemingly senseless events can be understood as grist for the mill of soul-making and deep healing," and "part of the value of suffering . . . is that it initiates or intensifies the search for what is most sacred."[5] Pain is our birthright. If we deny it we're robbed, we're cheated out of being human.

Our pain feeds our art. By transforming darkness into luminescence, we become better poets, writers, storytellers, and seekers. We become better people. We learn to make a work of art of our lives. When we have room for our pain, we have room for the pain of others, and we can actually help bear the suffering of others. Our suffering is a gift.

Through our suffering and healing, we help to enlighten humanity as a whole. Healing comes about through a change of consciousness, a change of heart; through forgiveness of others and ourselves; through forgiveness of Life and forgiveness of God. Healing comes when we let go of how we *think* our life should have unfolded and, instead, accept our life the way it is. Through sorrow, you will bring more meaning, joy, and fullness to your life.

NUMBING OUT

I want to know if you can sit with pain, mine or your own,
without moving to hide it or fade it or fix it.
—ORIAH MOUNTAIN DREAMER

Instinctively, we try to shrink away from pain. Pain is messy and ugly. We don't have the time for it, and what will the neighbors think? So we pop a pill; we numb out; we coast. We've become experts at easing our pain, erasing any jagged edges, and pretending that dark nights of the soul don't really exist.

In the 1950s, when people visited their doctors because they couldn't bear the burdens of life or were feeling an emotional malaise, they were given a tranquilizer. There were so many people hooked on that drug that it became part of our culture. Today, anti-anxiety and antidepressant drugs are being prescribed with a vengeance.

Not long ago, I read an article on depression in a national magazine. The writer focused was on the new drugs available to curb this devastating disease. While some people have legitimate biochemical disorders of the brain, we need to consider that others may be experiencing their dark nights of the soul, and have been increasingly so over the past two decades. There is enormous pressure to do more, be more, make more. We spend more time commuting to our jobs and less time with our families. It's a fast-paced world, and every day we're reminded that we've got to stay current and flexible in order not to become obsolete. Stress is causing us to disconnect from our Spirit and feel fragmented. It's no wonder then that depression is on the rise. We've reached rock-bottom. And we're choosing to numb out with powerful drugs.

While I know that some drugs are necessary for some people, I also believe that as a society we're hooked on them—both the legal and illegal kind. "We get the message of pain all wrong," says Norman Cousins. "Instead of addressing ourselves to the cause, we become pushovers for pills, driving the pain underground and inviting it to return with increased authority."[6] Drugs are disempowering. And they are addictive.

Perhaps these heart-wrenching experiences come to teach us that joy and sorrow are two sides of one coin. You can't say "yes" to one without also saying "yes" to the other. Open your eyes to your dark nights of the soul. What is their lessons in your life? What wisdom do they bring? What healing do they offer?

A HELPFUL EXERCISE

When you have a moment to reflect, take out your journal and answer the following questions:

- What dark night of the soul have you experienced?
- What signs are there in your personal or professional life that may be symptoms of a dark night of the soul?
- What dark night of the soul might you be going through right now?
- What do you think the "gift" is?
- How might the dark night of the soul feed your art?

RESPECT AND RELEASE YOUR FEELINGS

We know too much and feel too little.

—BETRAND RUSSELL

One February several years ago I could not get out of bed for three days. Sadness engulfed my heart. I felt I had been betrayed by a friend, and all I could do was cry and try to sleep. The depth of my sadness was so real and so overwhelming that, quite frankly, part of me thought I was going crazy. I could hear a voice in my head saying, "My God, Grace, get a grip!" But when I tried to deny how I felt and force myself to get up, I would fall back into bed, completely limp with sorrow. Eventually, a deeper voice—my higher Self—reassured me, "It's okay; you're not going crazy. Just stay with it. Respect your sadness. You'll figure it out."

I did figure it out eventually. Yes, I was upset and hurt by the incident, but I came to realize that most of the emotion I had felt and released in those three days had been an "old" betrayal from my childhood that had been locked away in my body. When I was two years old, my parents left me with my grandparents in southern Italy so they could take advantage of employment opportunities in Switzerland. They had felt extremely guilty about leaving me, so, to avoid the pain of separation, they had left after putting me down for a nap. When I woke up, they weren't there. Intellectually, I've always understood why they did it. But emotionally, I felt tricked, deceived, and betrayed. I had carried all that childhood sadness inside my heart until the day my sense of betrayal was triggered again, this time at a deep level.

Swiss-German psychotherapist Alice Miller says it is not childhood trauma per se that engenders problems later in life, but our repression of the feelings associated with the trauma. Feelings are repressed when the child has no one to name, listen to, and validate his or her feelings. Given no language and no voice, the fear, anger, and rejection are banished to the realm of the subconscious. "But they will, nevertheless, stay in her body, her cells, stored up as information that can be triggered by a later event," writes Miller in *The Drama of the Gifted Child*.[7]

We must overcome this disease of repression. We need to respect our feelings, not hide them. We need to release them, not bottle them up. Once we become conscious of our pain, we must go through it and cry our tears, express our anger. When your feelings come out in full force—whether directed at yourself, your partner, or your children—know that old feelings from the past are asking to be healed. Pay attention to them.

Expressing feelings is as natural as walking or eating. But we've been conned. Too often we are told that men shouldn't cry and that women shouldn't get angry. What the mind represses, the body expresses. Unexpressed feelings from the past stay locked in our cells and block our vital energy flow.

Research suggests that many conditions and illnesses are linked to an inability to express feelings and emotions. Releasing emotion is a blessing; it's an opportunity to heal the past. After my workshops, people will sometimes hug me. I usually let Spirit guide me and will often offer some words of encouragement or inspiration. That's when I see their eyes getting moist. Embarrassed, they stare at their feet. They apologize. I tell them, "Never apologize for your tears. Your tears are my gift to you." Every time you respect and release your emotions, know that you are healing a part of your past. You can let go of what was holding you prisoner and look towards taking the step towards your future.

RESCUE YOUR HEART

Keep knocking, and the joy inside will eventually open a window and look out to see who's there.

—RUMI

Imagine a treasure buried deep beneath the earth. To get to it, you must dig a tunnel straight down. You must work and sweat. Your fingers will bruise and bleed. You must burrow beneath the clay and the rocks. But the effort will be worth it, because you will find what you were looking for at the end. You'll find a treasure chest, and inside the chest will be your heart, bursting with infinite Love and Light. You were given this heart by your Creator to show love. But your fault lines, your dark nights of the soul, and the wounds from your past have prevented you from sharing your heart with others. It has been waiting for you to rescue it.

What makes this effort hard is that you must dig through five layers of old emotions and heal them before you can get to the love in your heart. Each layer of rock and sediment you clear away represents a different level of healing. The five levels of healing are Anger, Sadness, Fear, Longing, and Forgiveness. You will come to know each level intimately by naming it, feeling it, and expressing it. Every time you shed a tear, express your anger, feel your fear, or admit a longing, you are getting closer to being able to express your love. But in order to love, you must rescue your heart. Healing happens when we embrace all of our emotions, feel them, and then let them go.

It's easier to move through those five layers if you can think of a specific example that triggers each feeling. Is there a relationship that needs healing, perhaps with your mother or father or a past lover? Is there a trauma you must deal with? What is a burning issue in your life right now? What relationship would you like to heal?

Emotions are stuck energy; they are communications or expressions that were not allowed to surface. As children, adults do a good job of shutting down our tears and our angry outbursts. This accumulation of energy is stored in our cells until it creates imbalance and disease. I've noticed that people who cannot take action and move forward are people who are emotionally clogged. Chances are if you're feeling stuck in some area of your life; you probably need to unstick yourself emotionally. Once your *e-motions* are allowed to move freely again, the positive energy in all areas of your life is restored and your creativity returns. At least this is what I have observed in my experiences with hundreds of clients.

Sometimes, people can't heal because they try to take short-cuts. Each emotion in the process is valid and must be released. The only way to free your heart and make it whole again is to do the necessary work. The only way to take the step and move forward in a significant way is do this very important healing. If done with integrity and respect, the process can be life-changing.

HEALING THE FIRST LAYER: ANGER

You will not be punished for having anger.
You will be punished by it.
—BUDDHA

Anger is your personal jet fuel. Healing the past cannot be done without respecting and releasing your anger. Anger is the top layer of dirt and clay. You can't get to any other level of healing without first cleansing your body of anger. Writing about your anger is one level of expression. But you also need to voice it. Scream, yell, swear, growl, roar. Let your anger free itself through your voice. Find a private place and trust your process. Next, you must rid your body of anger. It's been locked in your tissues and your cells. It's been clogging your energy. There are many ways to move anger out of the body—beat a rug, drive your fists into a pillow (in anger-release workshops, we use punching bags, or batting).

How do you know when all the anger has been cleared out of your system? You'll know when your recall of the event or trauma no longer triggers your rage. Clearing anger is not a quick fix, though. As with all emotions, be aware that you can spend any amount of time at each level, depending on the event or relationship you are trying to heal. For example, a friend of mine who was making peace with her abusive childhood spent two years feeling angry about everything. Don't judge yourself. Give yourself time. You may be digging for a while.

Women often skip the anger stage, despite the fact that most of them carry enough rage inside to blow up a football stadium. I have participated in anger workshops, and I lead women's weekends where people do deep process work. A room full of people releasing anger and pain through the voice and the body can often resemble a maternity ward! It always amazes me how people who appear to be quite meek and mild-mannered can store enormous amounts of anger within. It's those people who take longest with this first layer.

Make anger your ally. It will not betray you. Rather it will tell you when you have been betrayed by others. It will tell you when you have betrayed your heart. It will show you which rooms of your castle you have closed off. To get in touch with your anger now, get out your journal and think of a person or event that really bugs you, and then start writing. Here are some statements to help you with the dig:

- I feel angry when _____.
- How dare you _____.
- I hate it when _____.
- I resent that _____.
- I'm fed up with _____.

In the book *Anger Kills*, author Redford Williams says that by being angry with others you're killing yourself. We know that anger can hurt your health, but if left unexpressed, it also can hurt others, sometimes those we love most. Angry people are hostile and belligerent. As a society, we've paid a high cost for uncontrolled anger. It has showed up in our neighborhoods, classrooms, and homes. Listen to your anger and learn to express it in a healthy way. If this is your issue, get professional help.

Healing the Second Layer: Sadness

**We remember sadness so that we can ignite
and enhance life.**

—BRIAN SWIMME

To penetrate this layer, we must cry. We must feel sad. Unfortunately, this is the stage that most men avoid and where most women hang out. When women feel frustrated and angry, they cry. Men get angry. "Losing it" for women means crying. For men, it's a fit of temper. Men don't want to feel sad, because they've been trained to equate tears with weakness. If women must get in touch with their rage, then men must shed a few tears.

I had a client once who was so unaware of his feelings that he didn't have them in his vocabulary. He was a member of Mensa and prided himself on his intellectual abilities, but he also had been severely abused as a child. He had shut down his heart and his capacity to feel anything. I counseled him for years. When he cried his first tears, it was an epiphany. We had finally broken through the concrete wall surrounding his heart.

Think about the incident or relationship that you expressed anger at and now express your sadness about the same situation. Do this exercise in private, when you know you will not be interrupted. Don't let anything interrupt your tears. Let them flow out of your body like a peaceful river. Put your shame on the shelf and feel compassion for yourself. Hold your heart in your hand and envelop it with kindness. That's how you heal your pain.

I couldn't talk about certain events in my life without my lower lip quivering. That's how I knew I still had sadness left inside me. When you have cried all of your tears around a certain event or relationship, it's over. You're ready to move to the next layer.

Here are some statements to help you express your sadness:

- I feel sad about _____.
- It makes me sad when _____.
- It cuts like a knife when _____.
- I feel let down about _____.
- I'm hurting because _____.
- I feel sorrow over _____.

HEALING THE THIRD LAYER: FEAR

Fear is what blocks an artist. The fear of not being good enough. The fear of not finishing. The fear of failure and of success.

—JULIA CAMERON

I will talk about fear in detail in chapter 6, but the fear you are releasing at this stage is specifically about the situation you have selected to heal. Many of us have lots of fears that we are not conscious of. For example, Claire, one of my clients, had been abandoned by her mother when she was two years old and she grew up not knowing who her parents were. She had so much anger and hurt about this that she couldn't wrap her brain around fear. "Fear?" she would remark. "I don't have any."

It took a while, but Claire at last became aware of childhood fears she had experienced around the abandonment. "I was scared of being alone. I was afraid I wasn't good enough." And then she began to cry. I recognized that Claire still had sadness to express, tears to shed. Healing in one stage may trigger another, and that's okay. Some people while expressing their fear get in touch with their anger, and that's beneficial, too. That's why it's important that you don't rush through the process. Right now, focus on fear. Express it with your voice and with your pen.

- I'm scared that _____.
- I was afraid of _____.
- I'm frightened about _____.
- I'm worried about _____.

HEALING THE FOURTH LAYER: LONGING

It doesn't interest me what you do for a living. I want to know what you ache for, and if you dare to dream of meeting your heart's longing.
—ORIAH MOUNTAIN DREAMER

We all have deep longings, aches that yearn to be satisfied, depths that crave to be filled. When our desires and longings are not met, we grow bitter and resentful. This layer is an opportunity for you to state your heart's longing without compromise and fear. When you think about your relationship with your parents, what didn't you get? In your relationship with your ex, what did you want but never received? What do you need now from the significant people in your life?

Have you forgotten the longings of your heart? When my children were younger and I was away teaching seminars, I would call every night to speak to them. Those phone calls weren't always easy for me. As soon as Jasper and Kajsa came to the phone, their precious little voices would get straight to the point. "I want you, Mommy." That's all they'd say, over and over, like some sort of mantra.

"Tell me what you did today, my darling," I would ask my daughter.

"I want you, Mommy."

"How was school, Jasper?"

"I want you, Mommy."

The pain of their longing would cut right through me. I ached desperately to hold them, to smell them, to kiss them. Their longing for me was so strong and direct, and they could express it in such a straightforward and healthy way. Most adults can't do this because they're ashamed of their longings. They feel they don't have the right to them. To heal and get to your heart buried deep in the rock, you must awaken your deepest longings and desires. You may have shut down your longings as a child. What did you want but didn't get? This layer of healing is about acknowledging your unmet needs. Think about the situation you're working on and complete these sentences:

- All I ever wanted was _____ .
- I would have wanted you to _____.
- I want us to _____.
- I yearned for _____.
- I wish _____.
- I desire _____.

HEALING THE FIFTH LAYER: FORGIVENESS

When we forgive, we set a prisoner free and discover that the prisoner we set free is us.

—LEWIS SMEDES

Years ago I was invited to speak to a group of women who had been sexually abused. At one point I was speaking about the importance of forgiveness when a woman in the back row stood up and started yelling, "Forgiveness! You obviously know nothing about being sexually abused. I can never forgive that bastard for what he did to me. Forgiveness! How dare you come here and speak to us about forgiveness!"

I was horrified. I was still so green that I couldn't respond to her attack, so I backtracked and tried to suggest something else. Today I would have gone over to her with love and compassion in my heart and said, "You don't have to forgive. Forgiveness is for him. Letting go is for you. I am here to help you heal so you can move on with your life. When you've expressed enough anger, enough sadness, enough fear, then you'll be ready to think about letting go."

And then, to bring further healing to the group, I would have broken my own silence. "I know how difficult it is to consider forgiveness. I too was sexually abused as a child. I have similar scars. And yet I am here to tell you that forgiving him has made me free. I am free of the past and eager to embrace my future, and that's what healing is all about. I pray for that for all of you."

I was too ashamed to admit it then, but I can now. I'm amazed at how many men and women were sexually abused as children. Yet we still carry a lot of shame about it. We need to break the silence if we are to heal. We need to release those secrets from our past that keep us trapped. It is happening now. More and more people are naming their abusers and seeking justice.

Life is filled with hurts, both large and small. The only way we can walk away from the pain inflicted by others is through extending forgiveness. If you can't forgive, then let the hatred and pain go. The person you free is yourself.

This is the last layer to dig through before you can rescue your heart from inside the treasure chest, and it's the most challenging.

Why is it so hard to forgive? I think it's because it's difficult for our egos to let go of the power that comes from being wronged. As long as we feel hurt and damaged, we give ourselves the right to blame and judge. We are the victims. Ego can point the finger and feel a certain power. Forgiveness takes great strength because you are extending unconditional love to the person who wronged you. Unconditional love is possible only when we put our ego on the shelf.

There is also a difference between forgiving and forgetting. We may forgive, but that doesn't mean we forget. Forgiveness is an act of compassion, and compassion is holy. Forgiving someone's trespasses against us doesn't mean we forget about them; it just means there's no longer an emotional charge from remembering. Forgiveness doesn't mean the event goes away forever. It's still very real. It just can't hurt us any more.

Forgiveness is not just a gift you give the other person—it's a gift you give yourself. Open your Self to the possibility. Begin by completing these statements:

- I forgive you for _____.
- I forgive myself for _____.
- I understand why you _____.
- I'm letting go of _____.
- It's okay that _____.

Once you have rescued your heart, you can use it for its intended purpose—to love yourself and others. I offer this healing process as a way for you to release old emotion and heal your life.

TEN MOST COMMON QUESTIONS ABOUT HEALING

The following are the most common questions I get from people about how this process works:

1 How long does it take?

It depends on the issue you're working on. To heal each layer, it's necessary to remember events and past hurts and that may take time. Each person is different as is each issue that needs healing. There are no set rules. At my intensive retreats, it usually takes about two hours per issue, but I've had about eighteen hours to set the stage. If you're on your own, this work is rather difficult. You cannot do emotional surgery on yourself and then go and make dinner. I recommend taking an anger-release workshop, or finding a professional who will help you release old emotion. This investment may just be the most valuable thing you will ever do! Begin the journey by becoming aware of anything that is not right in your life right now; any unresolved issues or relationship undones. What pain are you harboring? Are you depressed? Anxious? Become conscious! This is your most important work.

2 What should I choose to work on?

Make a list of events or relationships that require resolution and healing. For example, you may need healing in your relationship with one or both of your parents, an ex-spouse, a sibling, a teacher, or an employer. Events that need healing might include your parents' divorce, your divorce, a death, a loss, a change, a trauma, an accident, a tragedy, abandonment, betrayal, or abuse. Choose the one that you would like to work on first and then proceed through the five layers of healing.

3   What's the difference between writing it and speaking it? Which should I do first?

I suggest expressing the emotion by writing it down first, then speaking it or yelling it and, for the anger stage, releasing it. One of the best ways to release anger is to roll up a bath towel and beat the bed with it. You also can buy a plastic bat and beat a pillow.

4   What if I can't get angry?

This is a common concern for women. We've not learned to get in touch with our anger, even though many women harbor intense rage. You've got to think about the event or the person who wronged you to get angry. If that doesn't work, go back to some of your anger statements and start saying them out loud. Choose a point on the wall or something else to represent the person you are thinking about. As you say, "How dare you? I'm so pissed with you!" the anger will start to rise to the surface. As soon as you feel it, start hitting the bed! If you're still having trouble with the anger stage, be patient. If after a while you still can't access your anger, I recommend taking an anger-release workshop. Getting anger out of your body could be the best thing you do for your health.

5   What if I don't express anger but I express everything else?

The reason it's so difficult to access our anger is that most of it is unconscious, especially the anger we felt as children. We've had to store it away, because it was not appropriate or, in many cases, not allowed by our caretakers. Left unexpressed, that childhood anger is still there and is activated by the people or events in our adult lives. Consequently, some people feel that anger is controlling their life. Remind yourself that anger is a legitimate emotion and part of who you are. You must give yourself permission to be angry. This is a therapeutic tool for healing. The anger you express is energy that must move out of your body.

6 What if the object of my anger is my elderly parent?

I know it doesn't seem kind to be expressing anger towards aging parents. They did the best they could to raise us, but the truth is, everyone makes mistakes and everyone gets angry. You don't have to express your anger to your mother in person. Do it alone, but do express it. Don't be afraid to feel it. Your relationship with your mother will be richer and more rewarding once you rescue your heart.

7 How often should I work on this process?

After you've finished writing, leave it alone for a few days. Then come back to what you wrote down and speak it. Releasing your anger or sadness can be exhausting, so after you do it for one issue, take at least two weeks before going through the process again for another issue.

8 How long do I beat the bed?

It is good therapy to get anger out of your body when you feel it. When you're done being angry, usually the body collapses and the tears come. As you enter the second level of healing, get in touch with your hurt by repeating your sadness statements. Stay with each level for as long as is needed. Another way to know you're done is read your anger statements. If you still feel a charge, you're not done. For some people, their reservoir of anger goes deep.

9 Should I do this process alone?

The writing is usually done alone, but when you speak it, especially when expressing your anger, you should do it with a professional or someone you trust with your secrets. I encourage you to find someone to work with to help you with this.

10 Why is it so important to express these negative emotions?

Remember, emotions are stuck energy. This accumulation of energy is stored in our cells until it creates imbalance and disease. If you want to take action and move forward, you must clear the emotional toxins that have accumulated over the years. Each trial, tribulation, hurt, or betrayal carries with it emotions that must be expressed. Many of us have pent up emotions from the time we were infants. All this repressed energy causes emotional, spiritual, psychological, and, in some cases, physical blockages. The process I'm suggesting is a tool I use at my weekend intensives for healing stuck energy. Almost everyone who has ever done this work with me, even the most skeptical, have always, *always* walked away feeling liberated. When you're ready, the right teacher will come. When you're ready, you, too, will free your heart.

HEALING OUR PAST RESTORES OUR FAITH

**All your past except its beauty is gone,
and nothing is left but a blessing.**

—A COURSE IN MIRACLES

Tom raised his hand; he wanted to talk about his marriage. He was worried that he was heading for divorce and wanted some advice. The seminar leader looked at him and said, "Well, my friend, the solution is easy—just love her." His argument was that *love* is a verb, not a noun, so all the distraught husband had to do was love her. Tom said that he couldn't, that he had nothing left to give. Again the seminar leader advised, "Just love her." Tom sat down again, embarrassed and confused.

The seminar leader's intentions were good, but Tom probably could not love his wife because his love is buried deep beneath layers of hurt, anger, and fear. Before he can feel love, he needs to rescue his heart. And to rescue his heart, he needs to express and acknowledge the layers of hardened and forgotten feelings. If Tom wants to save his relationship, he must first learn how to heal it. Until he can dig through all the layers of hardened emotion, his love for the woman he married will remain dormant, buried deep beneath the layers of rock and earth.

The truth is, we've all got emotional scars, but until we can look our past in the eye, it will always be telling us to be less than we can be. The Spiritual Age has a place for you to begin that healing process. Books beckon. Courses and workshops call out your name. Kindred spirits surround you.

We carry our own pain as well as part of the cosmic pain that binds our Spirits together. We're one family. When we have room for our own pain, we have room for the pain of others and we can actually help to bear their suffering. Only then can pain be transformed into joy. When an individual heals, so does the rest of humanity. And when humanity heals, so will the planet.

To grow your confidence and walk across that bridge towards whatever is calling you, you must heal the past—and rescue your heart. That is our greatest work, because that is how we nurture faith—faith in the Great Spirit, faith in others, faith in our dreams, and faith that the bridge will be there as we move towards our destiny. Emotional healing helps us restore our self-esteem. It helps us heal our bodies, minds, and Spirits. It allows us to cleanse our souls from the inside out, to throw open the doors in our beautiful castles. When we heal, we reclaim our magnificence. Our Spirit takes flight.

Healing past hurts can happen anywhere, any time. It can be triggered by a line in a book, a scene from a movie, a song on the radio, or a question from a stranger, if you're open and willing. Trust your intuition. When the time is ripe, you, too, will experience those holy moments; moments that heal the past, transform your present, and shine light on your future.

5

Esteem
Your Self

ST. PETER'S FOOT

**We are unhappy because we no longer believe we are
a special miracle . . . we have become cattle, numbers,
punch cards, slaves . . . we look in the mirror and no longer
see the God-like qualities that once were so evident.
We have lost faith in ourselves.**

—OG MANDINO

Should you ever visit St. Peter's Basilica at the Vatican in Rome,
you'll find the tomb of St. Peter himself, the humble fisherman
from Galilee who was one of Jesus' apostles. In front of the
tomb are ninety-five tiny lamps that stay lit the year-round. The
basilica is enormously captivating, and the first time I was there
I was awestruck by the grandeur of it all. The building houses
one of the world's most celebrated art collections, which
includes paintings, frescoes, and wonderful sculptures such as
Michelangelo's *La Pietà*.

"Follow this path and turn right. There you'll see a bronze statue of St. Peter. That's the starting point for the official tour, which starts again in half an hour," I was told by a Vatican tour guide. As I approached the statue, I noticed that St. Peter was truly majestic. He was sitting on a throne raised about four feet off the ground. He was cast in bronze, with exquisite detail, and wore a glorious crown studded with jewels and a robe made of red and gold silk. It was obvious that this was his church. As I got even closer, I noticed that below his robe his feet were not symmetrical. His left foot was perfectly formed, the toes intact, but the other foot, which jutted out a bit more, was totally worn away.

I remember thinking how strange this was. Why the imperfection? I stood back and watched as pilgrims and visitors from every corner of the world come to pay their respects and homage to St. Peter. They did this by kissing or patting St. Peter's foot! They needed to touch him, to hold on, to feel connected to this great saint. And then I was struck by how many millions of times St. Peter's foot must have been touched. Can you imagine how many rubs that foot must receive in a day or a year? The power of these constant caresses, like drips of water on rock, is so great that they can over time shape a substance like bronze or marble or granite.

When we're born, we're all given a huge rock of self-esteem. As children we love ourselves, we have faith in our abilities, and we know there isn't anything we can't do. There's not one tree we can't climb or sport we won't try or activity that's too hard. We jump fearlessly into the deep end of life. Kajsa's first word was "Self." I'd show her how to do something and she'd say, "No, Mommy. Self, Mommy, Self!" Indeed, children do have a strong sense of Self. It is powerful and magnificent to behold. But then they start to grow up and people come into their lives, just like the pilgrims in the cathedral, except that they don't all come to celebrate the child. Some come—unknowingly—to erode her rock. Some people rub just a little, so a bit of dust comes off, but there's no immediate damage. However, years of that subtle rubbing can do a great deal of damage. Others are more blatant; they come with their hammers and chisels and take big chunks out of the rock. That's called child abuse.

For many of us, the older we get, the smaller our rock. Bit by bit, day by day, our rock has eroded away. For some people, the big rock they were given at birth has been ground down to the size of a pebble.

WHAT IS SELF-ESTEEM?

**Self-esteem isn't everything; it's just that there's
nothing without it.**
—GLORIA STEINEM

What is self-esteem? Research done over the past thirty years has shown that self-esteem is our most important psychological resource. It is a powerful filter through which our experiences and perceptions pass. If that filter reflects a core of high self-worth, then the perceptions and experiences the individual has will be empowering and positive. If the filter reflects low self-worth at the core, then all the individual's experiences will be tinged with a sense of victimization and negativity. Self-esteem is like the moon. It waxes and wanes depending on our moods, the events in our lives, and how we handle them.

The man who first alerted the world to the importance of self-esteem, the father of the self-esteem movement in America, is Nathaniel Branden. In his book *The Power of Self-Esteem*, he defines self-esteem as "the experience that we are appropriate to life and to the requirements of life. More specifically, self-esteem is (1) confidence in our ability to think and to cope with the basic challenges of life; (2) confidence in our right to be happy, the feeling of being worthy."[1]

I was first introduced to the importance of self-esteem by Jack Canfield, co-author of the *Chicken Soup for the Soul* series. Through his company, Self-Esteem Seminars, Jack had been bringing the message of self-esteem to corporations and schools and to professionals in the field. Every summer he held week-long intensives for practitioners and facilitators who were interested in learning more about self-esteem. I attended the program during the summer of 1994.

Jack belonged to the first-ever task force convened to promote self-esteem and personal and social responsibility in California. I was impressed that politicians were behind the self-esteem movement, at least in some places. I learned that California was one of the few states to recognize the importance of teaching self-esteem to children and young adults. The task force had found that almost every problem of society, including violence, family breakdown, and drug and alcohol abuse, can be traced to low self-esteem. Its research showed that between 80 and 90 percent of five-year-old children have high self-esteem, but that by the time those children are ready to graduate from high school, their self-esteem has dropped dramaticically. Only 5 percent of adolescents feel sufficiently worthy and confident to handle the challenges that life presents. In other words, kids are born with huge rocks of self-esteem, but by the time those kids have grown up into adults, their rocks have been crushed. The result? Only one out of three adults has positive self-esteem.

This information produced a strong emotional reaction in me. I was simultaneously sad and angry. "What happened to those kids? Why did they stop believing in themselves? How did they lose that sacred connection to their magnificence?" I wondered. How could I teach adults to get it back? How could I teach teachers, parents, and corporate leaders to enhance self-esteem in people rather than tear it down? I felt the call to do something. Life is too short not to have the self-esteem we need to do the things we want. I wanted to help those who felt beaten down by life, discouraged, and perhaps lost. I wanted to reach out to all those who felt broken and teach them that they could feel whole again.

When I got back home, I was excited. I learned everything I could about self-esteem. If I was going to empower others, I had to understand it myself. What I learned is that self-esteem is a huge topic and everyone has an opinion on it. But to me, self-esteem has two components: self-confidence and self-respect.

Self-confidence is the part I link with the idea "the bridge will be there." This is the faith that, no matter what life sends you, you'll be okay; your bridge will be there. It is a deep knowing or belief that at the core you are a beautiful, radiant, and worthy human being who deserves love and happiness.

Self-respect I link with "take the step." This is the action we need to take in order to move our lives forward. This is where we act on what we know; we walk the talk; we take risks. We respect ourselves when our actions are congruent with our thoughts and beliefs. Without action, no integrity. No integrity, no self-respect. And no self-respect means no self-esteem. We need both self-confidence and self-respect in order to have self-esteem.

Perhaps one of the reasons that the self-esteem movement has received some negative publicity is that the focus has been too much on building self-confidence at the expense of building self-respect. That is the greatest challenge for teachers everywhere. How do you get people to apply what they know? This is my challenge when I give workshops and training seminars. I have found that for the most part we know what to do, but we don't do what we know. Learning isn't learning unless we can integrate it into our lives and take risks, make changes, do something different that will move our lives forward.

For example, we all know about the dangers of cigarettes, yet we smoke. We all know that junk food is not good fuel for the body, yet we eat it. We may believe we deserve happiness and love, yet our actions betray us. We all know the benefits of exercise, yet we don't exercise. The betrayal of integrity and the guilt we feel when we don't do what we know feeds into the negative cycle. We feel bad for not taking action and then that bad feeling keeps us stuck.

You can grow your rock of self-esteem by either working on your thoughts (faith) or by taking risks (action). It's a bit of a catch-22. You need to take action to feel good about yourself, but you need to feel good about yourself before you will take risks. There may be some situations in which you're comfortable taking risks, but in others, you might have to do some mental preparation beforehand. Remember the dream that opened this book? I tried to scale the sheer marble wall, but I couldn't do it by action alone. I kept trying, but I kept failing. I changed tactics. I paused, thought about it, then visualized and psyched myself up. Then my action was effective, and I got to the top. Action and faith must work together to grow self-esteem if we are going to be able to secure the future we want for ourselves.

What happens when we fail? I find that for some of us, if we take action and fail, the setbacks make it harder and harder to get back up and try again. Self-doubt is insidious. The only way to deal with self-doubt is to build a bridge of faith. You do this by changing the pictures inside your head, by challenging your core beliefs and your mental maps. The other way you deal with failure is by stumbling forward, not backward (I will talk about this in chapter 6). Let failure help you refine who you are. Don't let it stop you from taking action or taking risks. If you fail and learn from it, you're still moving forward. That's what is important.

HOW THE ROCK IS CRUSHED

So long as we are blind to our inner tyrant, we blame an outer tyrant, some person or some system that is victimizing us.

—MARION WOODMAN

Before we work on improving our thoughts and growing faith, let's examine that "inner tyrant." Do you criticize yourself incessantly? Do you have a negative tape inside your head playing over and over: "How can you be so stupid?"; "You'll never amount to anything"; "You'll never lose this weight"; "You're such a loser!" The fact is that many of us have childhood wounds. If our role models shame us, criticize us, and abuse us when we are children, it is difficult to feel worthy as adults.

We all have emotional "stuff" deep inside us from our childhood that affects our outer lives. Some of us—most of us—don't even know that stuff is there. When I was in my early twenties, I knew people who liked to immerse themselves in tranquility tanks to meditate on their stuff. I was intrigued. I used to think, "Wow, I wonder what stuff I have that I'm not aware of?"

Let's face it, we've all got scars. People who can nurture self-trust, self-respect, and self-love in their children are mature, responsible, and secure. They love and accept themselves and feel safe and secure in the world. But some parents, though full of good intentions, can place appalling roadblocks in the way. While you were growing up, did you ever hear these self-esteem-eroding words?

You're stupid.
What will people think?
You're no good at anything.
So you got ninety on the test. What happened to the other
   10 percent?
Bad girl! Bad boy!
How come you're not as pretty as your sister?
You'll pay for this!
Why would anyone want to give you a job?
I told you so!
You'll never be happy.
Why can't you be more like your brother, or the neighbor's
   children?
I wish you had never been born.
I wish you would just shut up!
You better stop eating, or you'll never attract a husband.
You're just a girl.
You're too much! I can't handle you!
You're driving me crazy!

Do any of these comments resonate with you? These are rubs on the rock of self-esteem. Over time they will erode children's confidence and make them believe that they are less than the spiritual beings they are. And what of the children who have more than verbal abuse heaped on them? Those are the children who are threatened and beaten regularly, shamed publicly, violated sexually—who have had to experience what I call the ugliness of life. The ugliness of life is what Oliver Twist experienced—hardship, cruelty, darkness, hunger, cold, loneliness, and betrayal. If this is what happened to you, then your rock of self-esteem has been torn asunder by a jackhammer.

Maybe you've said some of those things to your kids. People repeat patterns of speech and behavior they have learned. Patterns are repeated if there is no awareness there to defeat them. Don't beat yourself up about it; focus on the future. A wise woman once told me that with children, every day is a fresh page. You can create new memories by deciding to behave differently tomorrow.

Parents aren't always the villains. Sometimes the experts of the day are to blame for how children are treated. In Barbara Goldsmith's biography of Gloria Vanderbilt, she writes that the most eminent child psychologist in the 1930s was recommending total detachment in child-rearing—no hugs, holding, or kisses. Toilet training was to be completed at six months, and "spoiled" babies who did not comply were to be force-fed castor oil. Such "experts" help to erode our rocks. Parents who have healthy self-esteem have a strong sense of Self. They listen to and value their own instincts rather than blindly follow the advice of experts.

When our rocks of self-esteem are small, we haven't the necessary faith to cross our bridges. We don't believe in ourselves. We don't think we can do it. Sometimes we get brave and head out for the bridge, but the fear-monsters inside our heads are too loud. They hold us back and, month after month, year after year, those dreams on the other side of the bridge lie there dormant. We wait. "Maybe one day I'll have the courage." "Maybe one day I'll win the lottery." "Maybe one day Mr./Ms. Right will find me." "Maybe one day I'll be happy." And so we fool ourselves into thinking that by waiting for others, our happiness is secured; by waiting for others, we might eventually get the outside validation that we're okay. We don't take the step across the bridge, because our belief systems are flawed. We have lost faith in ourselves. We believed those who called us stupid and bad. Bit by bit they clipped our wings, and we stopped flying.

BROKEN ANGEL

Why have you valued yourself in pennies when you are worth a king's ransom? Why did you listen to those who demeaned you . . . and far worse, why did you believe them?

—OG MANDINO

I was at a conference in California a few years ago. While shopping one evening, I noticed some items on a half-price table. Immediately my eyes went to a stunning seraphim angel that had been marked down. I picked it up and noticed a label: "Broken—half-price." "Wow! It's beautiful," I thought. Though I looked carefully, I couldn't find the flaw. I took it to the counter and asked the sales clerk to show me the break. She too could find nothing.

"Maybe it was put on the table by mistake," I said.

The clerk went to the back room to ask her manager. When she finally returned, she said, "My manager said that if it's on the half-price table, then it's on sale."

"What about the break?" I asked her.

"My manager says if it's marked 'broken', then it's broken. Do you still want it?"

"Yes, yes, I'll take it!"

Were you labeled "broken" at some point while growing up? Were you humiliated and dumped on a half-price table for all to see? Were you awkward at something? Not good enough? Too much trouble? Did some adult calculate your worth and give you a price tag? Those labels are rubs on your rock of self-esteem. Who was ignorant of your magnificence?

Sometimes we may feel like broken angels, but we're not really broken at all. There's nothing wrong with us, but the labels from the past are a heavy burden. We've convinced ourselves that they were right after all. Those labels bruised our spirits. They were the voice of authority that as children we felt we couldn't challenge. But you can now. "Never in all the seventy billion humans who have walked this planet since the beginning of time has there been anyone exactly like you," writes Og Mandino in *The Greatest Miracle in the World*. "Never, until the end of time, will there be another such as you."[2] Appreciate that you are unique. Even your flaws and imperfections are unique. That is what esteeming your Self is all about. It's about realizing that you've had wings all along. You, my friend, can fly.

Dannion Brinkley was clinically dead for twenty-eight minutes after lightning struck a line to the telephone he was speaking on. It took him two years to learn how to walk and feed himself again. Fourteen years later, he had another near-death experience when he had emergency open-heart surgery. While he was "clinically dead," Brinkley had some amazing insights. He wrote *Saved by the Light* and *At Peace in the Light* to share the wisdom he received while on the other side.

Once we begin to really understand that we are not from Here, we are from There; that we all chose to come Here and were chosen to come Here; that we were somebody and something long before we came Here, only then do we comprehend that we are not poor, pitiful, stupid human beings. We are all great, awesome, powerful, and mighty spiritual beings![3]

If you could connect to your spiritual genesis, to the fact that you have wings, you would no longer suffer from low self-esteem or lack of self-worth. You would realize that who you are at the core cannot be harmed by anyone. That is what I think Jesus meant when he said in the Gospel of Thomas, "If you bring forth what is within you, what you bring forth will save you. If you do not bring forth what is within you, what you do not bring forth will destroy you."[4]

If you could bring out your intrinsic worth, your Light, your divine Essence, then you would be forever empowered to take the step and cross whatever bridge needs to be crossed in your life. Your rock of self-esteem would be solid. Sometimes a near-death experience, a spiritual encounter, or a wake-up call of some kind is enough to show you that you are an angel sitting on a huge rock of self-esteem. All you have to do now is fly.

Remember that when you put yourself down, whether consciously or unconsciously, you are denying your magnificence, denying your spiritual origin. And when you deny your magnificence, you give others permission to do the same. Self-esteem is plastic. If we become aware of our hurts, learn to feel our pain, and heal it, we become whole again. And when we're whole, we feel worthy. Your rock of self-esteem is your birthright. It is your ticket to everything you want in life. It is the foundation of your happiness. Once you love yourself and feel worthy of love, you will know who you are; you will understand your divine origin. The miracles of the Spiritual Age will start to shower stardust over your head.

YOUR THOUGHTS CREATE YOUR REALITY

Everything we are is the result of what we have thought.

—BUDDHA

Thomas Jefferson, founder of the University of Virginia and the third president of the United States, was also the principal author of the Declaration of Independence, which was signed on July 4, 1776. His good friend John Adams (the second president of the United States) defended the declaration before Congress. Both men proclaimed that they wanted to be alive for the fiftieth anniversary of independence. It was their vision and their dream. They nurtured this desire by returning to it often in their thoughts. Some would say it was a miracle, but on the morning of July 4, 1826, fifty years after America's Declaration of Independence, both men were still alive. Jefferson, who was eighty-seven years old, died after lunch that day, and Adams survived his friend by just a few hours.

This story amazes people. How was that possible? To reclaim our perfection and esteem the Self, we need to be aware of our thoughts. You are what you think. The Bible said it more eloquently: "As a man thinketh, so shall he become." So what do you think about?

Your thoughts have created the life you're living right now. Every single thought, whether positive or negative, the vision you hold of yourself or of your world—whatever you spend time thinking about—is the person you become. I don't want to say "the person you are," because who you really are is Light, Divine, Spirit. But negative thoughts can pollute this reality until you begin to doubt who you are and create a reality that says you're no good, unworthy, and unlovable. Whatever you consistently focus on mentally, you will eventually call into your life. Your thoughts may not be realized immediately, but eventually they do come to pass.

The creators of the movie *What Dreams May Come* explored the power of thoughts even after death. Robin Williams plays a character who dies in a tragic accident, as do his children. His wife cannot handle the grief, so she takes her own life. During the rest of the movie, Williams tries to rescue his wife from herself, from the hell she has created inside her head. While Williams is in Spirit form, whatever thoughts he has are instantly realized. The movie suggests that on the spiritual plane, where there is no body or physical mass to slow things down, as soon as you think it—*poof*, thought is realized. Thought is pure energy. In the movie, the new souls who arrive daily in this spiritual dimension quickly realize the speed with which their thoughts are actualized. They learn to monitor them carefully, lest they have an outcome they do not want.

Think about the thousands of thoughts you have on a daily basis. Are they positive visions of what you want, or negative, fearful visions of what you don't want? Suppose that everything you thought of, you experienced? Not next year, not next month, not tomorrow, but today. Right now. Would that motivate you to change your thinking?

Some research I read a while back suggested that on average we think fifty thousand thoughts a day, many of them automatic, programmed, and unconscious. What are you thinking about right now? According to the late John K. Williams in his book *The Knack of Using Your Subconscious Mind*, "Positive, constructive, purposeful, confident thoughts will gradually reproduce themselves in the actual conditions of a person's life."[5]

Throughout history all sorts of mystics, philosophers, and spiritual elders have warned us about the power of our thoughts. In *Conversations With God*, God tells the author, Neale Donald Walsch, "It is the time lapse between thought and creation—which can be days, weeks, months, or even years—which creates the illusion that things are happening to you, not because of you."[6] That is why people don't connect their thoughts with what happens to them: It's because of the time delay. They feel victimized by the events in their lives, not realizing that their thoughts could have contributed to the outcome. At another time God says, "Thought control is the highest form of prayer. . . . Therefore, dwell not in negativity and darkness. And even in moments when things look bleak—especially in those moments—see only perfection, express only gratefulness, and then imagine only what manifestation of perfection you choose next."[7]

People are indifferent to their thoughts because they underestimate their power to influence us. The truth is that negative thoughts not only block our energy, they block our ability to stay conscious and alert to the miracles of life.

KINESIOLOGY AND THE POWER OF THOUGHT

Take charge of your thoughts.
You can do what you will with them.
—PLATO

In some of my workshops I do kinesiology demonstrations. I find these an effective tool for showing people how powerful their thoughts really are. I've done them with all sorts of different groups, including once with a team of people whose members weren't getting along. They had many unresolved issues that led to manipulation and plenty of back-stabbing. Trust was low, but the senior managers needed the team to get along in order to ride out the many changes the organization was experiencing.

At the beginning of the workshop, I asked for eight volunteers to come to the front of the room. I told them to stand in a line facing the rest of the group and hold hands (a challenge in itself!). As I usually do in this exercise, I put a strong, hefty male at one end of the line to show that negative thoughts can disarm and weaken even the toughest of us. Then I proceeded to test his strength by having him extend his arm outward and telling him to resist my touch. I then pressed on his arm with only two fingers. His arm bounced up in a healthy display of power and vitality. I acknowledged his strength and told him to hold on, that I would be back.

Then I went to the person at the other end of the line and whispered in her ear, telling her to close her eyes and think one negative thought about someone in the room. She looked at me with a smile and whispered, "Ha, that's easy." I asked her to keep thinking that thought until I told her to stop.

While she was focusing on the negative thought, I went to my strongman at the other end of the line. Because they were all holding hands, an energy exchange was happening. I told him I wanted to test his strength again, while the woman at the other end of the line, seven bodies away, was thinking a negative thought about someone in the room.

That was when his Ego became thoroughly deflated. He held out his arm. I pressed with exactly the same pressure, and his arm was visibly weaker. You could see the shock on his face. His look said, "What have you done to me?" In some demonstrations I have done, the change is so visible that the audience gasps. It really is powerful.

I then asked the woman to erase that thought and to think of a positive thought about herself or someone in the room. I asked her to focus on that thought so that it would become emotionally charged. While she was doing this, I went back to the muscleman at the end of the line and tested his strength again. He was, of course, once more brimming with strength, but the look on his face was still one of confusion. I then sent them back to their seats and asked them to discuss in small groups what they thought had just happened.

Thoughts Lead to Destiny

You must declare who you are in public. Public declaration is the highest form of visioning.

—NEALE DONALD WALSCH

As I was explaining the power of thought at a seminar I was teaching in New York City, a woman in my audience got very excited, throwing up her hand, and crying out, "Oh, oh, oh! I get it, I get it! Oh, oh, oh!" She stood up and told us that she had heard something really powerful on the car radio that morning, so powerful that she had to pull over and write it down. She said she had never done such a thing before, but what she heard was so compelling she knew she had to capture it in writing. And now, after hearing me speak about the power of thought, she understood what she had written so much better. She was so excited that she could barely keep from jumping up and down.

By now all of us were curious, so I asked her if she would share with us what she had written. She reached into her purse and proudly pulled out a crumpled piece of paper, then stood up in front of two hundred people and read:

Be careful of your thoughts, because your thoughts become your words.

Be careful of your words, because your words become your actions.

Be careful of your actions, because your actions become your habits.

Be careful of your habits, because your habits become your character.

And be careful of your character, because your character becomes your destiny.

There was a hush in the audience. It was a powerful moment. She looked up at me and said, "Thank you, Grace. I get it. It all starts here," pointing to her temple. "It all starts with my thoughts, and I can change my thoughts." This was obviously a major shift in her thinking. It was one of those perfect teaching moments, when someone sees the light and shares it with others. Everybody wanted to write down the wisdom she had heard that morning, and I've been using it ever since. If you want to change your life, change what you say to yourself. Change the pictures inside your head. You can do this by activating your imagination.

ACTIVATE THE POWER OF YOUR IMAGINATION

Imagination is the first step toward action. You have to be able to hope before you move forward. Otherwise, you are always acting out of fear.
—GLORIA STEINEM

Imagination is a powerful tool. Take for example, falling in love. When love is new, we spend endless hours imagining what to wear, how we will be seen, what they will think of us, etc. We see the world through the filter of our lover. Everything we do, see, touch, taste, or experience, we experience through our beloved's eyes. We consume endless energy thinking, musing, wondering what it will be like when we are together. After a date, imagination embellishes and enriches the experience. This is imagination's role—to make life richer and more textured. A compliment can be turned over and over in our imaginations until it becomes an empowering mantra. A look or a gesture can nourish us for weeks, a deep, penetrating kiss for months and months. I know people who can still remember—that is, imagine—their first kiss. Even the thought of it can produce a flushed face and embarrassed looks. That's the power of imagination. Then when we fall out of love, it's because reality has in some way contradicted our imagination.

When I was traveling through India, I met a gentleman from England. He was visiting for the first time since moving away as a young boy. With tears in his eyes, he told me how disappointing his trip was proving, how betrayed he felt. It seems the India he remembered as a boy—the India he had spent hours boasting about to friends back in England—was nothing like the India he was experiencing during his visit. Reality didn't match the pictures inside his head.

The uncle of a friend of mine was reunited with his only sister after forty years. The visit back home to Greece was an experience he had imagined and looked forward to for a lifetime. He had lived in South Africa for most of his life and had told his children endless stories of his sister—of how they had grown up with no mother, of their trials and tribulations. The only family history he could give his kids were stories from his imagination, from what he remembered of his childhood and growing up with his sister.

Imagine then the disappointment when experience didn't match what he had pictured. He had never considered the possibility of a personality conflict between his sister and his wife. He had never imagined the worst heat wave in twenty years, which made being outdoors unbearable and tested everyone's patience. He had never imagined his sister arriving late at the airport to greet him. It was an unfortunate series of events, but the visit that was supposed to be the trip of a lifetime, the long-awaited reunion with a beloved sister, ended on a sour note. After he returned home, my friend's uncle fell into a deep depression, from which he never quite recovered. Sometimes when reality doesn't match our imagination, we feel cheated, betrayed. Our enthusiasm for life wanes. But sometimes imagination can also save us. It can be the only vehicle we have to escape from unbearable circumstances and painful memories.

CREATE A NEW VISION

The primary function of the human being is to imagine, not to stand up straight, not to make tools and fire, not to build communities or hunt and till and tame, but to imagine all these other possibilities.

—JAMES HILLMAN

The musician Ray Charles was totally blind from glaucoma by the time he was seven years old. If that wasn't enough of a hardship, he was orphaned by the time he was fifteen. He started playing the piano when he was five years old, and while at the school for the deaf and blind, he spent hours teaching himself to play by ear. He dropped out of school when he was fifteen and started performing with small bands, doing gigs in local bars and hotels.

When he was sixteen, Ray Charles borrowed six hundred dollars and took a bus to Seattle. When people later asked him why he chose Seattle (it wasn't exactly the music capital of the world), he replied that he had wanted to get as far away as possible from Florida, perhaps because he had so many bad memories of the place. So he consulted a map and chose Seattle because it was the farthest away. When he got there, he used the last of his money to hire a few musicians and formed the Ray Charles Band. One year later, he hit the big time. Today his CDs sell on average half a million copies. Many people have asked him how he did it, considering all the obstacles he had to overcome. You know what he says? "I saw myself as a recording-artist star. It was the image inside my head that pushed me forward and kept me going. I saw myself as a star, and so I became one."

Ray Charles's imagination helped him create another reality for himself. Sometimes our thoughts come in the form of pictures. What picture of yourself do you carry around in your head? This picture is called your self-image or self-concept. The image is influenced by how other people treated you at an early age and the conclusions you made about that treatment. Psychologists believe that by age four you have a clear sense of whether the world is a nurturing or a hostile place, whether you are loved, and whether you're smart or dumb, capable or incapable.

Some people were treated badly and drew negative conclusions: "The world is a bad place. I'll never get what I want, because life is a struggle and I'm not worthy." Others were treated badly and yet for some reason they took it as a challenge. Their conclusion was, "Okay, so life is tough. But I'm not going to give up. I'll show them." They focus instead on what they want, and the pictures inside their heads support their final goal. In Ray Charles's case, his goal was to be a star, and that's what he became. What you must realize is that who you are today is not just a result of the way you were treated, or the obstacles you faced, but of how you internalized it—what you told yourself about what had happened to you—and how you behaved as a result. Think what would have happened if Ray Charles had thought, "Wow, I'm blind. I guess I'll never amount to much."

Decisions we make at an early age about who we are end up being strong indicators of our personalities later in life. Unless we consciously challenge the pictures of ourselves we have inside our heads—in other words, our self-image or self-concept—there can be no personal growth. What about you? Were you listened to? Did people respect your opinion? Were you treated like someone special, or were the people around you indifferent to your magnificence, your talents? Was your community of friends and relatives loving and accepting? Were you trusted? Were you loved for who you were? Were you celebrated?

Imagination is wonderful. It nourishes us spiritually. It creates dreams and fantasies that we have every right to. It feeds our souls. And while it's important to dream big, to focus on positive thoughts and outcomes, and to have faith in endless possibilities, we need to remember that sometimes our imaginations will let us down. But that's only because we have expectations. I know it's difficult not to enter the realm of expectation when you dream up futures for yourself, but leave yourself open to something better, God's plan, destiny, endless possibilities, or however you wish to think of it. Ask the Universe what lesson is there for you if the future is less than what you imagined. Imagine the *you* that you would be if you had the necessary self-esteem and faith to cross your bridge. Conjure up the highest thought you can think about yourself and then cradle it in the palm of your hand. That is who you really are. Forget the rest. Forget the fears and the voices from the past. You have the opportunity to take the step and become the *you* of your imagination.

TAP INTO YOUR SUBCONSCIOUS MIND

The conscious mind may not know how the subconscious works or feels, but the subconscious knows, to the last detail and shade of feeling, just what is in the conscious mind.

—JOHN K. WILLIAMS

It's only in recent years that we have come to appreciate the importance of the subconscious mind and its role in our creativity, energy, and success. By learning to tap into this underused resource, we can take action towards our goals, feel more confident and relaxed, and enjoy greater creativity and well-being. We know that important discoveries and works of genius seldom come from the conscious mind. The German scientist Hermann von Helmholtz, speaking to a group of friends on his seventieth birthday, said, "Happy ideas come unexpectedly, without effort, like inspiration . . . they have never come to me when I was at my working table." Henri Poincaré described the same phenomenon when he said that his creative ideas did not come to him while he worked at his desk, but frequently flashed into his mind while he was engaged in other activities. Charles Darwin, who developed the theory of evolution, wrote, "I can remember the very spot in the road, whilst in my carriage, when to my joy, the whole solution came to me." Einstein recalled that the unique relationship between time and space and the nature of reality sprang into his mind while was confined to his bed because of illness.[8]

The subconscious mind is a huge reservoir of all our past thoughts, attitudes, and desires. Into its trillions of pigeonholes go the things we read, hear, and observe; the pictures we see; the impressions we receive; the thoughts we entertain; our dreams and our feelings. It is on duty twenty-four hours a day. It has immense powers to solve whatever problem the conscious mind gives it. The subconscious mind is there to help us cross the bridge. It is our silent partner in life. It can help us achieve any objective.

Two key aspects to remember about the subconscious mind are: (1) it has the power to create, and (2) it can learn to obey the conscious mind. Unlike the conscious mind, it has no power of choice. It does what it is told. Its purpose is to create whatever is desired by the higher, conscious mind.

Our personalities are not static. We are not limited by the kind of person we were yesterday. We are constantly changing, and we can create ourselves anew each day. We can use the subconscious mind to give us greater faith in ourselves by directing it toward positive thoughts. "The first requisite of creative mental life," says John K. Williams in *The Knack of Using Your Subconscious Mind*, "is positive thinking. Aspiration molds the mind in a stronger way than does fear or trepidation. Appreciation is more creative than aversion. Confident thoughts are more powerful than questioning doubts."[9] By being aware of our subconscious self-talk and reframing our thoughts to be more abundant, more hopeful, and more positive in nature, we can create miracles in our lives. It's those thoughts that create the bridge to your dreams.

What do you say when you talk to yourself? What do you think about? That tape in your head, is it positive or negative? Most of us are not aware of our negative subconscious self-talk. It has been programmed since birth—even, some say, since the time of conception.[10]

Your subconscious mind hears everything you say or think. At the University of Michigan researchers flashed information cards for a thousandth of a second and then asked the hundred people who were participating in the study what they saw. Each person was hooked up to a monitor in the next room that measured brain activity. At the precise moment the information was flashed, even though no one felt they "saw" anything, their charts registered brain activity. What this tells us is that the subconscious mind is an incredible sponge. It soaks up impressions, messages, and information without our even knowing it. So even when the hundred participants couldn't recall an image, their brains picked up information. An imprint had been made.

Advertisers know how the subconscious mind works. That's why they pay networks big bucks, sometimes millions of dollars, to air their television commercials. Print ads are just as powerful. And if you think that magazines, newspaper ads, and billboards don't affect you, think again. There's something called subliminal messaging, and it's very powerful. When I was a university student, I attended an unforgettable slide-show presentation by Dr. Jean Kilbourne. She had just completed her PhD thesis on the subliminal effects of advertising and was eager to share her findings with students around the world. She went on to win international awards for her documentary *Killing Us Softly* (available in most libraries) and later wrote the book, *Can't Buy Me Love: How Advertising Changes the Way We Think and Feel*. Her work continues to remind me that no one is immune to the power of advertising. Today I share Dr. Kilbourne's research with people in my workshops. We all need to know how subliminal advertising seeps into our subconscious mind and to acknowledge that advertising in general may be contributing to our core beliefs and values without us even realizing it.

It's critical that we become aware of our thinking and learn how to harness those thoughts that go astray, that are self-defeating, critical, and negative. What negative core beliefs have limited your growth and stunted your potential? What were you told of your ability while growing up? Your belief in your ability is one thousand times more powerful than your ability. That's why, if you convince yourself of your limitations, your negative qualities, your less than human attributes—congratulations, they're now yours. Your subconscious mind listens to every thought or word you say and then delivers.

CONQUER YOUR NEGATIVE SELF-TALK

If everything you tell yourself about yourself becomes a directive to your subconscious mind, then any time you make a statement about yourself that is negative you are directing your subconscious mind to make you become the person you just described—negatively!
—SHAD HELMSTETTER

The following are just some of the things that we say or think about ourselves. You may think that they are innocuous thoughts, but I would like you to consider the person you might be today if you reframed some of these limitations to be less restricting and more empowering. How different would your life be? Put a checkmark beside the statements that relate to you.

☐ *I'm just not a patient person.*
☐ *I will never learn that.*
☐ *I can't seem to get organized.*
☐ *Today just isn't my day.*

☐ Nothing ever goes right for me.

☐ That's just my luck.

☐ I'm so clumsy.

☐ I'm just not creative.

☐ I can't do that.

☐ Everything I eat goes right to my thighs.

☐ It's just no use.

☐ I can't remember names.

☐ I'm not very good with details.

☐ I can't function without my first cup of coffee/cola.

☐ I will never lose these extra pounds.

☐ I never have enough time.

☐ I can never afford the things I want.

☐ I just can't seem to get anything done.

☐ Why should I try? It'll never work.

☐ I've never been any good at that.

☐ I never win anything.

☐ I feel like I'm over the hill.

☐ Nobody likes me. Nobody respects me. I'm a loser.

☐ I never get a break.

☐ That's too complicated for my simple brain.

☐ I get sick just thinking about it.

☐ Sometimes I just hate myself.

☐ I can't speak up. I'm shy.

☐ I never know what to say.

☐ Nobody wants to pay me what I am worth.

☐ I always get a cold this time of year.

☐ I'm just no good at math.

☐ I'm just not a salesperson.

☐ I hate my job/boss/co-workers/teachers.

REFRAME YOUR NEGATIVE
PROGRAMMING

**Become a possibilitarian. No matter how dark things
seem to be or actually are, raise your sights and see
possibilities—always see them, for they're always there.**
—NORMAN VINCENT PEALE

Why is it that our minds turn toward negative thoughts more
easily than to positive ones? Why do people gossip? Why do we
like to read about grisly murders, slow down to look at an accident, or watch violent TV programs? Our ancestors enjoyed
gladiatorial games in which people butchered each other in the
name of sport. As a journalist, I was amazed at the appetite people have for negative news. In fact, if it wasn't negative, it wasn't
considered "hard news." If you were a serious journalist, the
last thing you wanted to report on was "fluff," those feel-good
stories that I always seemed to gravitate towards (that's how I
knew I wasn't a "serious" journalist).

Some people believe that we grew into our negativity over
the course of human evolution. It may be a survival trait,
because it can help us prepare for potential dangers. The problem is that the pendulum has swung too far. Some people have
let a pessimistic attitude overwhelm their lives; all they see, all
they look for is the negative outcome. However, this perception
can be changed with intentional awareness. You don't have to
throw up your hands in despair when faced with negative voices
from the past.

The answer is "reframing." Reframing changes the way we
perceive what happens to us. We learn to give the events in our
lives a different interpretation so that we can call upon healthi-
er ways to respond to our environment. You might be thinking

that would be difficult to do, but it can be quite simple. Here's an example:

A client of mine suffered stress from his highway commute to work. He drove more than two hours every day during rush hour. During that long commute he would stress himself out over all the "bad drivers" on the road. By the time he got to work, he was in a foul mood and his staff had trouble relating to him. Not only that, but his wife was worried about what the aggravation was doing to his blood pressure. His inability to control his perceptions of the other drivers was stealing quality from his life.

Reframing for him meant that he had to tell himself something different about the bad drivers he saw on the way to work in order to produce fewer stress hormones in his system. So he learned to perceive them with new eyes. When a driver cut him off, he would create the following internal response: "Okay, buddy, I know, I know. You've got to get to the hospital because your wife is having a baby. Hey, I understand. I'm a dad myself." He imagined every bad driver was rushing to some emergency. Once our brains perceive a different reality, we experience different emotions. He could forgive the other drivers more easily when he gave them reasons for their mistakes. The result of this exercise was that he started to calm down and began letting go of his road rage. He stopped looking for the bad drivers.

Reframing is powerful. It can change your life. Think about a challenging relationship or situation you are dealing with right now. Ask yourself, "What attitude shift can I make that will allow me to see this situation in a different way, in a more positive light?" Think about this question. Ponder it. If you don't get an immediate answer, that's all right; the answer will come. How you see the world affects what you get from the world. If what you've been getting is not what you want, then you need to change your perceptions. Examine your filters. Do you have an optimist's filter or a pessimist's filter when you look at life? If you want to influence your level of happiness and inner peace, you must be willing to look at the way you perceive reality.

L + P = HQ

What is replenishing? What is depleting? What takes? What gives?
What wrings you out and truly, what rinses you with happiness?
—FRANCES MAYES

L stands for Life, P stands for Perception, and HQ stands for Happiness Quotient. Life happens to us. Think about the things that happened to you today. Were you late for work? Did you yell at your kids? Were you stuck in traffic? Did you celebrate a birthday? Were you criticized or praised today? Was your plane on time? Did the meeting run late? Did someone stand you up?

Did you make love? Have a fight? Shop? Pay a bill? Meet a friend for lunch? Play with the kids? Cut your finger? Divorce your spouse? Quit your job? These are just some of the events that happen to people every day. You can't always control *life*.

HQ is the happiness quotient. Are you content, or are you wanting? Are you satisfied with the decisions and choices you've made, or do you feel an ambiguous emptiness in the pit of your stomach? Do you feel connected to your joy and your Spirit? Have you accomplished your heart's desires? Think about it—are you happy? The happiness quotient is the outcome, the bottom line. It changes over time; we have good days and bad, valleys and peaks. How we feel about what's happened to us depends on the P in the formula.

P stands for perception, the way you perceive what happens to you. This is where you have the power and ability to influence your happiness quotient. We know that stress is not the event itself, but comes from how you perceive the event. Therefore, you have the power to control your stress levels by altering your perception, by reframing what happens to you. You can choose to see the world through an Optimist's Filter (OF) or a Pessimist's Filter (PF). If you see the world through an Optimist's Filter, you approach life from the point of view of abundance. You believe the world is a good place. Before reacting to events, you stop and think and decide on the best course of action. You feel empowered and proactive. You know that life is a series of choices and that the word "responsibility" means the ability to choose a response. You don't blame the outside world for your problems; rather, you look within and ask yourself, "How can I avoid this mistake next time? What can I do now to make it better?" Optimists can have bad days, but they bounce back quickly. They are future oriented.

On the other hand, if you see the world through a Pessimist Filter, you react negatively to everything. You believe the world is a hostile place, and you spend a lot of time being afraid and angry. You perceive the events of your life through a "poor me" filter. You exhibit the classic victim's outlook, blaming everyone and everything around you for your troubles. Because of your negativity, you look outside yourself for validation, and when you don't get it, you feel unworthy and afraid to take action. When a pessimist has a bad day, it can turn into a bad week, a bad month, even a bad year. Pessimists have trouble shaking off misfortune.

Your filter—whether PF or OF—will make a huge difference in how you perceive the events of your life. It's what we tell ourselves after the fact that causes the stress or the negative feelings. In other words, it's not the experience but what you choose to do with the experience. So many of our problems are unnecessary. We cast events as problems when they don't need to be. If only we knew how to come up with different interpretations of what happens to us. That is the secret behind stress management—indeed, behind life management. Event control is about interpretation, and interpretation is based on how we perceive the event. As the philosopher William James said, "The greatest discovery of my generation is that humans can deter the courses of their lives by altering the attitudes in their minds." Your attitude is your interpretation, the spin that you put on the events in your life. Your happiness depends on you. When reframing the events life has sent you, keep the following points in mind:

THINK POSITIVE ABUNDANCE

Why gaze down the sewers when there is loveliness all around us?

—PARAMAHANSA YOGANANDA

When you think abundance, it means that you focus not on what you don't have, but rather on what you *do* have. This thinking is at the core of a positive attitude. Canadian artist Doris McCarthy, who is ninety-three years old, says, "I keep my eye on the half of the bottle that is full and ignore the half that is empty. The half that is full is so rich, so rewarding, so happy, that I would be stupid to regret the things I haven't had."[11]

Choosing to look at your glass of water as half-full rather than half-empty is not about denying the truth; it's about shifting the focus to an attitude of abundance rather than an attitude of need. Abundance thinkers are optimists; they have a higher threshold for change, transition, and stress. Furthermore, they live longer than pessimists.

Thinking abundance is simple for some people. They automatically see the silver lining in every cloud. Sometimes we make fun of those people, thinking them unrealistic, stupid, or naïve. Optimists have their bad days, too. They grieve; they cry; they get angry. But they eventually bounce back, because they're resilient. Unlike a pessimist, they refuse to stay stuck in the problem and blame the past. They would rather focus on the future and figure out what action they can take.

Job placement agents tout a positive attitude as a necessary survival skill for the future. Realize that stress is a perception, not an event. Whatever the situation, reframe it to focus on abundance—on what you have, rather than on what you don't have. Keeping a gratitude journal may help to get you in an abundance mind set.

FOCUS ON WHAT YOU WANT

**When I have forgiven myself and remembered who I am,
I will bless everyone and everything I see.**

—A COURSE IN MIRACLES

Reframing the negative things you think or say to yourself is
not about denying reality; it's about focusing on where you
want to go. If your job requires you to remember names, for
example, and you're not good at it, telling yourself that you're
bad at it will not help you. Something more empowering would
be to think, "Remembering names is sometimes difficult, but I
am getting better and better at it" or "Remembering names is
hard, but I can do it." This attitude moves you from "stuck" to
"unstuck." It's breakthrough thinking.

Psychologist James Loehr helps to train athletes, among them
tennis great Martina Navratilova. Loehr has studied what tennis players do during a match in the twenty-second break
between points. He found that mediocre players use that time
to scold themselves for mistakes they've made during the game.
Champions spend the time focusing and preparing their minds
for the next point. One focuses on the past, one on the future.

Tell your brain what you want. Create the vision and see it in
your mind. Don't think of all the things that could go wrong;
that is called "catastrophizing." Focus instead on how you want
it to turn out. Let's say you have a job interview, an important
meeting, or a big event coming up. Instead of anxiously thinking about everything that can go wrong, focus instead on how
you want things to go. Use all your senses to see the final result.
Feel the emotions you want to feel. Talk to yourself in a way
that will support the end result you want. Avoid using language
that is fearful, self-deprecating, and self-defeating.

WATCH YOUR LANGUAGE

And I made a rural pen,
And I stained the water clear,
And I wrote my happy songs
Every child may joy to hear.

—WILLIAM BLAKE

When reframing negative thinking, you must realize that the subconscious mind does not register negative words such as "don't." For example, if I said to you, "Don't think of a purple turtle," what would immediately come to mind? A purple turtle, right? The subconscious brain works this way, too. It ignores "don't" and focuses on the other words. So if you say to yourself, "Don't be stupid," "Don't get angry," or "Don't be late," what have you just programmed yourself to do? Be stupid, get angry, and be late, of course.

When I went to the playground with my kids, it used to break my heart to hear the adults saying, "Jimmy, don't break your neck"; "Don't fall down"; "Don't hurt yourself." What was even harder to bear were the negative statements predicting some dire future outcome. "Billy, you're going to fall from up there!" or "Samantha, you're going to kill yourself and give me a heart attack!" I'm sure I must have sounded like an alien, because I was yelling things to my children like "Jasper, focus"; "Be careful"; "Concentrate"; "Kajsa, good girl. You can do it!"

CHALLENGE YOUR CHILDHOOD ECHO

Each of us has the right, possibility to invent ourselves daily. If a person does not invent herself, she will be invented. Be bodacious enough to invent yourself.

—MAYA ANGELOU

Think back to your childhood and some of the things that were said to or about you. Were they positive or negative? Adults are not always enlightened. I think we get too caught up in describing behaviors we dislike rather than communicating the vision we want. One of my clients, Bob, recently told me that he didn't like school when he was a kid. One day his principal came to his home and told Bob's parents, "This boy will never amount to anything." Luckily for Bob, he didn't let that opinion decide his future. He went on to a teachers' college and eventually became a school principal himself. Twenty-five years later, at a class reunion, he met his old principal and had the last laugh.

What were you told when you were growing up? Perhaps you remember wonderful things being said to you. Those positive statements may have planted seeds that you are today reaping. Maybe you weren't so lucky. Perhaps, like Bob, you were given negative pronouncements, prophecies on how badly you would turn out. Did you let them come true, or did you defy them? Sometimes, by becoming aware of childhood statements— the echo from the past—and challenging them, we can plow through our fears and anxieties and take the necessary action.

Here's an example. When I was a kid, my mother used to say to me, "You'll never find a hat for that crazy head of yours." I guess she was trying to say I was too intense, too much, too restless. The message I received was that I would never be happy: I wouldn't be able to find a man I could have a family with, or the right career, and so on. I have defied this message and found many hats to wear, and I feel blessed to be who I am. I also realize that when I was younger, I might have been offended by the word "crazy," but not now. To me it's a compliment. It means that I am creative, energetic, and passionate. I think outside the box. I recognize this and take pride in it. Think of an echo from your childhood. If it was positive—great! Affirm it. If it wasn't—challenge it by looking at it from a different angle and finding the positive in it.

RAISE THE BAR

We ask ourselves, who am I to be brilliant, gorgeous, talented. . . . Actually, who are you not to be? You are a child of God. Your playing small does not serve the world.

—MARIANNE WILLIAMSON

I once heard a story about a rug seller. A man who had taken part in looting a city tried to sell one of the precious rugs he had acquired. "Who will give me a hundred gold pieces for this rug?" he cried, throughout the town.

He found a buyer and, after the sale was completed, a comrade approached the rug seller and asked, "Why did you not ask for more?"

"More?" replied the rug seller. "Is there a number higher than a hundred?"

How often have you set your sights too low? So many of us are capable of so much more, yet we don't even know it. We have set self-imposed limits on ourselves. In many cases, we have sold ourselves short. When you think about yourself, raise the bar. Use your imagination to create the grandest, most magnificent vision of your life that you can possibly have.

I once had a client in sales who hired me to motivate her team. She kept saying over and over that she believed that the bar was set too low, that their results could be higher. Even though she believed they could do better, most members of the team felt there wasn't any more they could humanly do. She was convinced that if they could just remove the limit inside their minds and raise the bar higher, they could jump over it into new possibilities and more success. She was right. We found that what was holding her people back were assumptions made by their previous boss who quit when the organization restructured. Slowly with awareness, they pushed beyond those assumptions and, with her help and faith in them, generated more success.

Be open to trying on new glasses, new hats, and new ideas. Stretch yourself. Take some risks. Aim higher. Don't settle. So many of us settle, like the eagle that hatched with a bunch of chickens. Every day he would walk out with his adopted brothers and sisters and play in the dirt. Occasionally, he'd look up and see one of his relatives flying high in the sky. "Wow, I wonder what kind of bird that is? I wish I could fly like that." He was born with wings made to soar, but he never knew it. If he had flapped them around a bit and taken a risk, he might have realized he could be something more than a chicken. That's what happens to so many of us. What a tragedy to die not knowing we have wings.

Esteeming your Self is about treasuring your infinite depths. It is about celebrating and releasing your splendor. It's about connecting to your beauty, intelligence, and radiance. When you believe in yourself, you feel invincible. If life sends you challenges, you bounce back; you find another way. Esteeming the Self is about believing in yourself because your *belief* in your ability is one thousand times more important than your ability. When self-esteem and positive self-worth rise within us, our mental bridge becomes real. Once we can see the bridge and feel it there beneath our feet, we step across it with confidence. We take action *expecting to succeed*. Expectation is a critical component for successful action. If you act expecting to succeed, you will. If you act expecting to fail, you will. When we esteem the Self, we strengthen our ability to expect excellence from ourselves, and our action steps become effective. Action is what it's all about—not just dreaming our dreams but *act*-ualizing them.

Reflections and Helpful Exercises

Do not allow your life to represent anything but the grandest version of the greatest vision you ever had about Who You Are.

—NEALE DONALD WALSCH

1. Learn to Reframe

i) Choose some negative statements about yourself that you checked off on pages 180–181. Write them down in your journal.

ii) Now ask yourself what underlying message each statement supports. What core belief lies beneath this negative statement?

iii) Ask yourself how this core belief may be sabotaging you. How is it stopping you from having faith in yourself so that you can take action? If you can think of specifics, great!

iv) Rewrite the statement, keeping in mind the pointers on how to reframe negative self-talk (think abundance; focus on what you want, not what you don't want; use only positive language). Your reframing statement should sound empowering but ring true for you. You don't want to deny your reality, but rather to suggest another possibility for your brain to consider. Play with it.

Example 1

  i) Statement: "Nothing ever goes right for me."

  ii) Underlying message: "I'm a loser; I can't do anything right."

  iii) How does it sabotage me? It prevents me from taking risks because deep down I believe I won't succeed.

  iv) Reframing statement: "I attract positive experiences that add value to my life," or "Everything happens for my highest good," or "I learn and grow from every experience."

Example 2

  i) Statement: "I can't seem to get organized."

  ii) Underlying message: "I'm out of control; I can't cope. Help!"

  iii) How does it sabotage me? I'm constantly stressed and over-whelmed by life. I'm tired, crabby, and impatient with everyone.

  iv) Reframing statement: "I am becoming better organized day by day," or "I have enough time to accomplish my priorities," or "I am in control of my time."

Write the reframing statements on index cards (these can also be called "declarations" or "affirmations"). Writing them down gives them more weight in your subconscious mind. Remember how teachers used to make us write lines if we misbehaved? I once knew a boy who had to write "I will not speak out in class" one thousand times. I'd like to meet him today! Visualize the pictures that accompany your reframing statements. Hear the statements inside your head when you need them most; they will become your invisible cheerleaders. You can also tape-record your positive statements and listen to them as you're drifting off to sleep. This is effective for subconscious reprogramming.

The most important thing is that *you* create the vision of the person you want to be. You are the producer, director and actor in the movie called *Your Life*. You are in control. Make a commitment to empower yourself. Erase the negative programming from the past. Tell yourself, "I am attracting people and experiences that celebrate me and that allow the best version of myself to emerge. I am a magnet for all good things. I draw to myself abundance and opportunity. I radiate love and goodness to all I meet. I am a channel for divine Love and divine inspiration." You become what you tell yourself.

2. Choose Your Theme Song

What soundtrack is playing inside your head? Do you have a theme song, like Ally McBeal in the popular television series that starts playing at odd times? Depending on your level of self-esteem, your theme song might be upbeat and cheery or dark and somber. Is it serious music or inspirational? Is it the theme to *Chariots of Fire* or *Rocky*, *Star Wars* or *Friday the Thirteenth*? Is it a jazzy instrumental or pop? Classical or reggae? Sometimes we play scary *Friday the Thirteenth* music when we're having a *Chariots of Fire* day. Why is this?

Music has the ability to cut through to the subconscious mind and release endorphins. It can be used as a tonic to affect your mood, and it can also assist you with your goals. I recommend choosing a piece of music that makes you feel invincible, that is the best version of you. I need to immerse myself in music so that it penetrates my every pore. I can't bear to hear my favorite songs reduced to background music.

Crank it up. Let it seep into every part of your body. Let it make love to your soul. Close your eyes and connect to your power, your magnificence, your invincibility. Then turn the song off and think about that undone that is beckoning you from across your bridge. Is it a conversation you need to have with an ex? Is it a new job? Is it starting over with someone new? Is it public speaking? Whatever it is, close your eyes and imagine it. Feel the sensation in your body. Once you've got it firmly in your mind, turn your theme song back on. Associate the feelings of your theme song with the difficult thing you have to do. Imagine facing your demons and doing that thing with courage, commitment, and Love. Imagine the outcome you want—not the one you fear might happen, but the one you desire—all the while listening to your song. Eventually, any time you experience a crisis of faith, you will be able to close your eyes and connect to your theme song.

3. Connect to the Future You

Sit in a comfortable chair and close your eyes. Take three deep breaths and relax. Spend a few minutes breathing deeply and imagining yourself on a beach, relaxing under the sun's warm rays. Then visualize yourself in the future when you're old and gray, the day before your death. Imagine that you have lived a great life filled with rich experiences and adventures. Your heart is filled with compassion and wisdom. Then think of a situation or problem in your life right now that you can bring to your future self for illumination and guidance. Ask the older version of you for help with this problem or issue. Be aware of the first thought that you have. If you don't understand it, ask your future self to explain. Engage in a dialogue. There's no telling what insights you might gain from an older, wiser version of you. Capture it afterwards by writing it down.

4. Have a Gratitude Journal

Keep a special journal next to your bed just for your gratitude thoughts. Before retiring each night, write down five things you were grateful for that day. For example, "Today I am grateful for (1) the telephone conversation I had with my parents this morning, (2) the surprise tulips from my friend Katalin, (3) the warm wind in my hair as I walked Jessie tonight, (4) the hugs my kids gave me when they got off the school bus, and (5) the delicious dinner my husband prepared."

By making a habit of gratitude you start to reveal the magnificence that is your life. Gratitude is healing. It helps us connect to what is really important. It helps us stay grounded in Love. It grows faith, and it builds strong bridges to possibilities not yet born.

5. The Worst Thing Someone Could Say to You

Write down the worst thing someone could say to you. Ask yourself why it hurts so much. What part of you does it violate? Then create a statement that not only contradicts it, but enhances it. For example, if the most painful thing someone could say to you is "You're out of your league. You can't do this," write down "I can compete with the best. I can do it. I can do anything!"

Some other examples: "You're stupid!" transforms into "I'm brilliant. In fact, I'm a genius!" "You're a loser" becomes "I'm a winner—everything I touch turns to gold!" These positive statements will eventually influence your core beliefs about who you are.

6. Exercising Your Rights

People with low self-worth have limiting or restrictive core beliefs. In some cases, they don't even allow themselves basic human rights, such as the right to be happy, the right to make mistakes, the right to create one's own life. They feel they don't deserve a second chance or don't deserve to be loved. These irrational thoughts are based on a poor self-image. To esteem the Self and grow faith, we need to examine and become conscious of our core beliefs. One way to do this is to become aware of our rights. The rights we allow ourselves determine the action we take.

For example, if you don't give yourself the right to make mistakes, then your actions will be characterized by perfectionism. You will work hard to make everything around you perfect. We all know that striving for perfection is a self-defeating exercise. I always tell people to strive for excellence, not perfection. Perfection is an unattainable and self-defeating goal. Not allowing yourself to make mistakes will eventually become a burden and a curse. Joy will be sucked out of your life.

Take a look at the list below. Which of these rights do you honestly feel you allow yourself? Which ones do you not allow yourself? Write down any other right that occurs to you. Then ask yourself, "Are these rights based on rational, realistic, empowered thinking or on irrational, unrealistic, self-defeating thinking? Which rights encourage self-worth?" The ability to be loving and kind to your Self is one of the first steps towards healthy self-esteem.

I have the right to

change my mind	be moody
be outrageous	be impatient
choose my own life	have my own opinions
create myself	hang out with whom I please
have a bad day	color outside the lines
have a bad hair day	play
be grouchy	cry
make a mistake	feel free to be me
be wrong	be loved
look awful	have feelings
feel like not caring	feel tired
choose my friends	lose my temper
be authentic	take a day off
relax and do nothing	speak out if I don't agree
seek meaningful work	

7. Create a Collage of Your Passions

This exercise enhances your self-concept and is a lot of fun, too. If you have kids, get them involved. Start collecting words, pictures, images, anything that speaks to you. Get a huge piece of bristol board and decorate it with your pictures, images, colors, or poems. Arrange them any way you want. Then post it where you can see it every day. Remind yourself of your splendor, your magnificence, and your Spirit.

8. Be Vigilant About Sights and Sounds

Avoid watching the television news just before going to bed. It pollutes your subconscious mind. It hammers at your rock of self-esteem. If you're that much of an information junkie, get your news earlier in the day via radio or print, which are weaker mediums. It's not necessary that you see and hear the wacko who raped and killed an eleven-year-old girl. It's not necessary that you see people running from bullets in war-torn countries. Those stories pollute the Spirit and subconsciously challenge our collective faith. Native cultures believe that we are all One, that the human family is connected on a spiritual level, so we are therefore psychically affected by the actions of others. How can our souls feel good when we hear of such stories? I'm not saying that you should lock yourself in a closet and hide from the world around you. Just be vigilant and proactive about the media content you and your family decide to take in. Young children are spiritually pure and impressionable. Let's prolong their innocence for as long as possible.

6

Activate Your Courage

BRAVE HEARTS

Life is either a daring adventure or it is nothing.

—HELEN KELLER

The tallest mountain in the world stands 29,000 feet above sea level. The air is so thin at the top that helicopter rotors cannot keep the craft in the air. If you flew from either Katmandu or the base camp straight to the summit, your lungs would explode. That's why the climb must be made gradually; climbers must spend several weeks, even months, at each camp. I learned these things when watching *Everest*, a documentary about three people who attempted the climb. They are an American man, a Spanish woman, and a Tibetan man whose father, Tenzing Norgay, was the first Tibetan to scale Mount Everest, with Edmund Hillary in 1953.

The most treacherous and challenging part of the journey is the last leg. Just before our three heroes set out to conquer this dangerous section, they get word that a violent storm the day before killed three other climbers who were attempting the summit. The news comes as a shock. One of the men who died had been one of the most experienced climbers in the world and a good friend of theirs. Would the storm still be raging when they get close to the summit? Should they attempt it or go home satisfied that they had almost made it? It is an agonizing decision, but they choose to be brave hearts. At midnight they set out on the twelve-hour journey to the top of the world, in total darkness and sub-zero temperatures.

As they get closer and closer to the top, their bodies weaken. Hunched over, faces almost brushing the snow, they find each step forward a painful ordeal. Their cumbersome arctic snow suits, the heavy equipment on their backs, and the thin air that makes breathing a grueling experience are all making these three adventurers move in slow motion. Watching them, I am stunned by the sheer strength of their will and the power of their desire. When physical exhaustion has almost swallowed them whole, something stronger keeps pushing them forward. When every cell in their bodies wants to scream, "Stop!" something else inside them screams even louder, "Keep moving!" "This is risk-taking; this is raw courage," I say to myself. The climbers stay true to their vision and are rewarded with a view of the world from the summit of the tallest peak on earth. They have conquered Everest.

Before you can take the step towards your dreams, before you cross your bridge, you must have a clear vision of what it is you want—your *desire*. To figure out what you want, you need to dig for your truth and uncover your authentic Self as we did in chapter 1. In chapter 2, we worked on creating a destiny mandala and a mission statement for yourself so you would have a better idea of where you want to take your life. In chapter 3, we looked at the role passion plays in our lives and in helping us to move forward. In chapter 4, we cleared blocked energy and unresolved issues from the past. In chapter 5, we learned about confidence and how to grow self-esteem. Now in this chapter, we will work on the final frontier—conquering fear.

When all is said and done and we have all the tools necessary to change our lives, why do we still not take the step? Why are we paralyzed? Why do we shrink back from what our soul came here to do? Fear—conscious fear, unconscious fear, mind-numbing fear, middle-of-the-road fear—it's fear all the same. Fear freezes us and makes us unable to move our lives forward. The antidote for fear is courage. Courage will take us across the bridge, but it also will help us to stay authentic and not betray our hearts. It is courage that allows us to express all the colors of our passion, and it is courage that will help us choose our destiny. The fact is that we need courage to stay optimistic when the rest of the world wants to drown itself in self-pity. That's why conquering fear is the last frontier.

Courage is the ability to face fear and take the step. Courage is feeling terrified but moving your feet anyway. Think of those times in your life when you were afraid, unsure, or anxious, yet you managed to find the courage to do what you had to do. "I want to know if you can get up, after the night of grief and despair, weary and bruised to the bone, and do what needs to be done to feed the children," writes Oriah Mountain Dreamer in her poem *The Invitation*.[1] Sometimes our fear seems all-pervasive, tyrannical, and overwhelming, yet something stronger pushes us across the bridge. You might be thinking, "No, not me. When I'm afraid, I just freeze."

To conquer fear, you grow courage. Courage is the art of feeling comfortable about feeling uncomfortable. Let's begin by defining courage.

Defining Courage

**To one who waits all things reveal themselves, so long as
you have the courage not to deny in the darkness what you
have seen in the light.**

—COVENTRY PATMORE

The *Oxford English Dictionary* defines "courage" in two ways:
(1) "a readiness to face and capacity to endure danger," and (2)
"an inherent freedom from fear."

Let's look at the first definition and break it into two parts.
First, "a readiness to face," which acknowledges that an undertaking is scary and risky but you're ready to do it regardless.
Most people would agree that the thought of climbing Everest
is a scary idea. What's a scary idea for you? What have you
wanted to do but were afraid to? For some people, contradicting their boss is a scary idea; for others, it's changing their
wardrobe, committing to a relationship, going to a Third World
country, or dealing with conflict. The willingness to face your
scary idea is the beginning of courage.

The second part, "capacity to endure danger," is what you
call upon within yourself to help you go through with the
action that makes you fearful. In other words, enduring the
uncomfortable feelings associated with doing something you
fear. This is what our three heroes had to do on the last leg of
their journey. The capacity to endure danger means that
although some things in life are going to be risks, you understand that risks are part of life. You take risks because you have
courage, because you want to live life fully. "The credit belongs
to the man who is actually in the arena," said Theodore
Roosevelt, the twenty-sixth president of the United States,
"whose face is marred by dust and sweat and blood, who

strives valiantly, who errs and comes up short again and again . . . because there is no effort without error and . . . if he fails while daring greatly, knows his place shall never be with those timid and cold souls who know neither victory nor defeat."[2]

Part 2 of the definition is "an inherent freedom from fear." Once upon a time there were knights and warriors who fought battles and whose courage was honored in lands all over the world. Every battle took hundreds of lives, yet each young soldier knew that fighting was part of his lot in life. They were fearless and stoic. Who has this kind of courage today? I find that most young children are fearless. They don't just walk across their bridges, they do somersaults across them. But for adults, fear remains a common denominator.

If we feel fearful, does it mean that we can't be brave hearts, that we can't be courageous?

Not at all. I believe that courage comes when we face the fear and do it anyway.

So many of us don't because we need to feel comfortable before taking action. Fear makes us feel uncomfortable. The objective is not to rinse your body and psyche clean of fear; the objective is to survive the fear while moving forward. That's courage. Make fear your ally. Make fear your friend and overcome your need to feel comfortable all the time.

"Facing it, always facing it, that's the way through. Face it," said one of Joseph Conrad's characters. Face the fear, but do what you have to do. Don't give up; don't run away; don't numb out. Stay in the arena and play. The Japanese have a similar philosophy. Their Morita therapy says, "Be scared to death, but still do what you have to do." We need to acknowledge the fear; to smell it, taste it, feel it—but still take the step. That is courage. That is the person who Roosevelt says "is actually in the arena."

FACING FEAR AND TAKING ACTION

Stop to look fear in the face. . . . You must do the thing you cannot do.

—ELEANOR ROOSEVELT

When were you most afraid and what did you do about it? Freeze? Run? Lie? I'm not talking about the kind of fear you feel when you have writer's block or when you're procrastinating about a decision you don't want to make or when you can't ask someone out for a date. I'm talking about gut-wrenching, life-or-death, fight-or-flight kind of fear. Have you ever experienced this kind of fear, when your life or the life of someone you loved was in danger? How did you behave? Chances are you stared fear down in order to survive, and not only that, you did what you had to do. You took action.

I was eighteen years old and living on my own in Paris, France, studying French at the Sorbonne University. It was late evening, and I was coming home from the library. While walking on Boulevard Saint-Michel, I sensed that I was being followed. I picked up my pace and finally arrived at my building, but it had one of those heavy steel doors that shuts slowly after it's been opened. I looked back down the circular staircase and saw three young men slip through the doorway just before it closed. My heart started pumping hard. "Oh, my God! They're after me," I thought. Should I run? My room was at the very top; I still had eight flights of stairs to go. "Why doesn't the elevator work at night?" I thought angrily. "Maybe if I stand perfectly still they might think I went through one of the other doors on the main floor." While all these thoughts were rushing through my brain, my feet kept going, up, up, up, round and round and round, trying to be as quiet as I could. My heart was pounding heavily. My legs were about to give out. I was getting dizzy. But I kept moving. I made it to my door, but the men had caught up to me. We got a good look at each other as I hurriedly turned the key and dashed inside. I was so scared I was shaking, but I managed to lock my door and push the big dresser in front of it. Then I sat on my bed, trying to catch my breath and feel my legs again.

Just as I was thinking, "I'm safe. I made it. It's okay," the young men started banging on my door and yelling at me in French. When that didn't work, they tried to cajole me out with sweet talk. Then they got angry and threatened to break my door down. I had no phone, and none of my neighbors was coming to my rescue. Eventually, after what seemed like hours, I couldn't hear them any more; but I was still too terrified to open my door. I never saw those men again, but I know that fear had made my feet move faster than I would ever have thought possible. My fear had saved my life.

I have noticed that the times when I was most afraid were also the times I felt most compelled to act. When faced with situations that threaten our well-being, we activate our "action" button. That's why human beings can sometimes perform incredible acts of physical strength and endurance in life-or-death situations. In those situations, we tune in to our warrior energy and do what we have to do. This reaction to fear is hardwired into our nervous system as a survival mechanism. It's called the stress response—we get fired up with hormones so that we can take action. In extreme situations, we usually have two choices: either we fight, or we take flight.

WHEN FEAR CLOUDS OUR THINKING

And since the root of all error is fear, only the undoing of fear will bring correction.

—PAUL FERRINI

Sometimes when we experience extreme fear, we lose our ability to think straight. Have you made any bad decisions because you were fearful? This happened to me the time I thought my sixteen-month-old baby girl had been kidnapped. I had hired as a nanny a woman who spoke little English but who loved children and seemed to be kind-hearted. After working with us for about a week, she said she wanted to take Kajsa for a walk in her stroller. It was a beautiful day, and I agreed.

Expecting that the nanny would walk up and down our street a couple of times and then return, I was surprised when half an hour had passed and there was no sign of her. After one hour had passed, I became alarmed. Where could she have gone? I went out to look, but there was no sign of them. With each passing minute, my fear grew more intense. Not only that, but my mind started putting together a case for why this woman would want to steal my baby and leave the country. I began to remember snippets of conversation—how she had tried to have a baby but couldn't, how she had always wanted a little girl, and how Kajsa was the most beautiful baby girl she had ever seen and that she even resembled her.

I looked at the clock. More than an hour had passed. Where were they? Suddenly I realized I didn't even have the spelling of the nanny's last name. "Of course, that way I can't trace her when she takes my baby out of the country!" I yelled to my husband, grabbed the car keys, and ran out of the house.

Every second that went by seemed like an eternity. What to do? What to do? Tears were cascading down my face. "This is what it must be like to go crazy," I thought. This was bone-chilling fear as I'd never experienced before. This was worse than any threat to my life—this was my precious baby. I stopped the car right in the middle of the road, got out, and started screaming like a crazy person.

My angels must have been out in full force, because a police cruiser just happened to be driving by while I was having my lunatic moment. The officer escorted me home and tried to reassure me that the police would do whatever they could to find my baby. Soon there were five cruisers in front of my house. A missing child is serious business.

The excitement brought my neighbors out to see what the commotion was all about, but I was in no condition to talk to anyone. I was in my blackest hour, experiencing a terror that I had previously never even imagined. How would I survive this? I walked onto the front porch in panic, and that's when I saw the nanny nonchalantly pushing my daughter's stroller.

I went inside to tell my husband and the police. Immediately, tears of relief streamed down my face. And then, almost as immediately, feelings of guilt and shame washed over me. "Oh, my God, what will the nanny think?" When she walked in, she was stunned to see the house swarming with police officers. As soon as she saw my face, she understood why.

"Where were you?" my husband asked her.

"I went for a walk. I stopped to do some shopping," she said. I was too weak to say anything. I grabbed Kajsa from her stroller and pulled her close to me. I looked at the nanny. How could I tell her that her lack of judgment had taken years off my life? That her two hours of shopping were the blackest two hours I'd ever experienced?

It was wrong of her to do her shopping during working hours and wrong of her to take my baby along. Nevertheless, had I not been so gripped with fear, I might have saved myself two hours of anguish and terror. I might have spent a bit more time looking for them. Had my judgment not been clouded over, I might not have built up such a convincing case for baby theft. But my fear swallowed me whole that day. It was brutal. Sometimes when fear activates us, it pushes the wrong button.

WHEN FEAR DOESN'T MOVE US TO ACT

Only those who dare to fail greatly can ever achieve greatly.
—ROBERT F. KENNEDY

There is another type of fear that I call "everyday fear," the kind that doesn't automatically activate the action button. What are these everyday fears? When you need to speak up or do the right thing but don't; when you should apply for a job, confront a friend, give a presentation, make a tough telephone call, go to work for yourself, or tackle an "undone" that has been demanding your attention—and you don't, then you are experiencing an everyday fear. Wouldn't it be great if our action button could be activated by this kind of fear, too? In addition to the fear of getting hurt, there are also fear of failure, fear of the unknown, and fear of success. If these everyday fears don't automatically activate the action button, how can we take action and conquer them? We do it with courage, love, and faith.

Taking action on these things is not a matter of physical survival, but of spiritual and emotional survival. To ignore the call from your soul, from the dreams that may be beckoning you from the other side of the bridge, or from a relationship that is important to you means that you never reach your potential, you never actualize your fullest being, you're never quite the empowered individual you were meant to be. What's at risk is your "aliveness." That's why the poet W. H. Auden says that all men die, but few really live. If your spirit withers away but your body is still walking around, are you really alive? That's a question that many people today are asking themselves. Do you opt for the path of least resistance? Do you coast? Do you run away from your everyday fears?

You might be reading this and thinking, "Gee, is that what happened to me? Is that why I turned off my passion for life?" Maybe. And then again, maybe not. As I described in chapters 1 and 4, there are many reasons why we turn off. Letting fear rule our lives and ignoring the call from our soul may be part of the reason. Especially at mid-life, many people seem to experience a sort of existential crisis when they come face-to-face with their mortality and the fact that time is running out. They look at their list of undones and are overwhelmed with regret and sadness. Fear can be an absence of courage, an absence of love, an absence of faith, or a combination of the three. When we can't or don't love ourselves enough or believe in our abilities, then we are incapable of taking action. Lack of action leads to feelings of failure and regret. Depression may set in, which can cause us to lose even more faith, love, and courage. And that's how the self-defeating cycle works. We don't activate our action button, because we're stuck in this negative cycle.

THE SELF-DEFEATING CYCLE

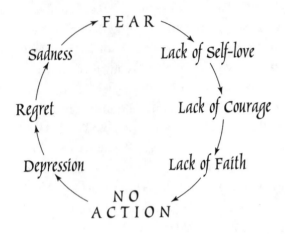

FEAR

Sadness

Lack of Self-love

Regret

Lack of Courage

Depression

Lack of Faith

NO
ACTION

BEFRIENDING FEAR

Where the mind is without fear and the head is held high,
Where knowledge is free . . .
Where tireless striving stretches the arms towards perfection . . .
—RABINDRANATH TAGORE

How can we take the step despite our fear? After all, feeling scared is not unnatural. Our tendency is to ignore the fear, hide it, or deny it. But fear needs to be understood and befriended if you are going to activate your action button. Learn to recognize fear as soon as it appears. Name it and locate it. Where, for example, do you feel the fear? For some people, fear lives in their stomach. For others, it lives in their legs. For others, it's a pounding in the chest. Where does fear live in your body? You need to recognize it, acknowledge it, and understand it before you can overcome it and activate your action button. Also ask yourself, "What is the worst thing that can happen?" Coming face-to-face with your worst fear is the first step in conquering its power over you.

Then, using all your senses, delve into your fear. Describe it. First, what does your fear look like? What color is it? What shape? If you could draw it, what would it look like? If your fear had a voice, what would it say to you? Write down all the things your fear would tell you. Next, what does your fear taste like? Be descriptive. Don't just say "awful" or "bad." Use expressive language. For example, "My fear tastes as putrid as a truckload of rotten eggs." Finally, how does your fear smell? Again, be descriptive. By getting to know your fear in such an intimate way, you can break out of it and take action despite the fear. It is no longer the monster you thought it was. By unmasking it, you will know what it is.

Once we've understood our fear, we can start to move through it. But for some people, understanding their fear is still not enough. They can't move forward, because they are plagued by feelings of hopelessness and inadequacy. The cure for hopelessness is faith. The cure for inadequacy is Love. We must learn to have compassion for ourselves and to accept ourselves despite our weaknesses. The greater our self-acceptance and self-love, the more action we will take. For some people, this is all they need to start taking small steps, but it's a bit of a catch-22. You've got to believe in yourself to take risks, but you have to take risks in order to believe in yourself.

Right now, let's activate the action button with courage. I'd like to help you start thinking like a brave heart. How can courage help us? The root of the word is the Latin *cor*, meaning "heart." So when we say "take heart," we really mean "have courage." "Courage" is also the root word of "encouragement." When we encourage someone, we are giving them reinforcement for their heart. Brave hearts are in contact with their fear every day, yet they walk through it. They take action.

JUST DO IT!

It is not because things are difficult that we do not dare, it is because we do not dare that they are difficult.

—SENECA

Courage allows you to swallow your fear whole and step across that bridge. You're scared as hell, but somehow you face the fear and move through it. That's what it means to "just do it." Courage lets you activate the action button by employing your own sheer will to break the self-defeating cycle. Everyone admires those who can just do it. That's why the Nike ads were so successful—they resonated with people. We want to do it, but we feel impotent. We often make it so difficult for ourselves. We procrastinate. We're scared. We blame it on perfectionism. We blame our circumstances on the weather, our parents, and our kids. We say we're not ready; we need to do more research or get another degree or additional credentials. We complain about all those things we still haven't done and yet we postpone taking action. When will we be ready to *just do it*?

When I lived in San Diego, California, I produced an afternoon radio program that went on air live from 3 to 6 p.m. I used to arrive early and start digging for good stories to feature. I'd hunt down articulate and lively speakers who could discuss the top stories of the day. I was always searching for what we called in the business "good radio"—people and stories that would touch the heart and add value to daily life. My search for the perfect show could have been endless. There was always one more telephone call I needed to make or one more lead to chase down. But every day at 3 p.m. I had to go to air with a show. There could be no more preparing or postponing. It was show-time. I was forced to *just do it*.

Wouldn't it be great if our lives worked like that—if at a certain time every day or week, our "producer" walked in and said, "Okay, enough procrastination. It's show-time. *Just do it!*"? If you were forced to do it, how would your life be different today? What have you been postponing? If you could do one thing that would move your personal life forward, what would that be? If you could do one thing that would move your professional life forward, what would that be? If every day you took a step forward, even if it were a tiny baby-step, eventually you'd be on the other side, eventually you'd accomplish your goals. Baby-steps accumulate like compound interest. The critical first step is to face your fear—recognize it, feel it, and endure it. Fear is uncomfortable, but it doesn't have to stop you from crossing your bridge. Take action, even if it's just a tiny step. This will grow your self-confidence, which will create courage in your heart. Once you feel courageous, you will be able to face more of your fears and take more risks and so on and so on. That's how brave hearts do it.

BRAVE HEART CYCLE

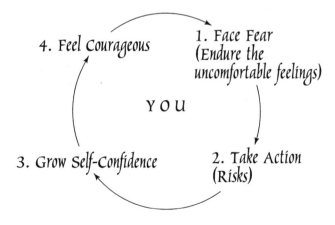

4. Feel Courageous

1. Face Fear
(Endure the uncomfortable feelings)

YOU

3. Grow Self-Confidence

2. Take Action
(Risks)

Eventually, you will have made it all the way across the bridge and accomplished what you set out to do. That will give you the confidence and courage to tackle more projects and cross more bridges. Imagine how different your life might be if you took consistent steps towards completing your undones instead of complaining about all the roadblocks in your way. In most cases, *you* are your biggest roadblock! It's your attitude. A colleague of mine is fond of saying, "We all know that the only problem in your life is *you*."

Sometimes we make crossing our bridges so difficult for ourselves. We think there is some complicated magical code that would make things a lot easier, if only we could crack it. The truth is that the magic is in you. All you need is a little push.

Make a list of what you want to do. Then ask yourself, "How can I break it down into small steps so I can begin taking action?" Action will empower you. It will grow your self-esteem. It will grow your faith. Action breeds courage, and courage helps you take more action. What small step can you take? Keep your eyes, ears, and heart open. I *en-courage* you to keep planting seeds—read, listen, and learn. Stay alert to synchronicities. They are the language of your Spirit guides and your higher Self. Don't let anyone tell you there is only one path to your calling. Even if your calling is the same as a friend's, your path to it will be different. Honor your uniqueness. Do not get hung up on having the right skills, credentials, degrees, or diplomas. If your soul is calling you to something, then you already have a natural talent for it. Believe in your cause, but most importantly, *just do it!* The rest will take care of itself.

COMPLETE YOUR UNDONES

We each have a finite number of heartbeats, a finite amount of time. But we have enough heartbeats and enough time to do what is important to our lives.

—SUSAN L. TAYLOR

Undones are signals from your higher Self that you have unfinished business begging for completion. You know it's an undone because when you think of it, it saps your energy. Undones are mental nags. They remind you that you have broken agreements with yourself. They rob you of your self-respect. They deplete you of creativity. They drain you of joy. Completing them brings internal peace and personal effectiveness.

Undones are unresolved conflict, withheld forgiveness, unspoken love, ungiven appreciation, dreams never carried through, goals not met, promises not kept, and tasks not finished. Do you have any of those? Undones come in all shapes and sizes and in every area of life. Some people have a whole basement full of undones. What are yours?

Relationship Undones

This is the biggest category of undones for most people. Do you have an unresolved conflict with anyone? Almost everyone I know has unfinished business with someone else: an argument that never got settled, a rumor that was never quashed, a conversation that we were too scared to have. Time passes. Life moves on, but the blocked energy remains. After the tragedy of 9/11, I read about a reconciliation movement happening around the world. Family grudges were dissolved, and relationships

217

became the glue that held us together. If you had minutes left, what would you say and to whom? It broke my heart to read the cellular messages left for loved ones from the planes that were hijacked. Does anyone in your life need to hear "I love you"; "I am sorry"; "I forgive you"? Do you need to write someone a thank-you note or show appreciation? Do it now, while it's fresh in your mind.

Make a list of the people with whom you have some unresolved issue. They can be living or dead. Then for each of them ask yourself what would it take for you to have a clean slate with that person. What healing do you need in order to cleanse yourself of the negative emotion surrounding that person? Maybe you need to have a conversation. Maybe you need to apologize. Maybe you need to let them know you've forgiven them. Maybe you just need to let it go.

When you think of your family, what's missing? What robs you of energy? A parent's death? A child's illness? A messy divorce? A love affair that had to end? What are your regrets? Have you lost touch with family? Are there family members in different countries that you would like to meet? Is your undone a family reunion that you keep talking about but never organize? Is there something you've always wanted to do with your family but haven't yet done? Perhaps it's the trip to Europe or the visit to Florida to see Mickey Mouse? Do you have practical undones, such as no will or life insurance?

Career Undones

Ask yourself whether you like your work or pine for a more rewarding career. Do you have some dream or goal that you have been too scared to think about? What did you want to be when you grew up? What was your fantasy career? Did it come true? It's never too late. I know people who started new careers in their forties and fifties and who are happy. The average person today will experience at least seven career changes. Are you ready for a change? Perhaps you don't have the necessary skills or experience. Are you developing your talents? Are you learning new things? Perhaps you like your work but feel burned out. Maybe you need a sabbatical. Perhaps you like your work, but you want to break out on your own so you can have greater flexibility and control. Our work is more than our livelihood. It's a way to connect to purpose. It's a way to share our gifts so we can make a difference. It's important that we feel good about it.

Financial Undones

When it comes to investments and finances, what are your undones? Do you save? Do you pay your debts on time? Are you planning for your retirement or your children's education fund? Are you saving for your dream house, a trip around the world, a sports car, a summer home? What financial undones do you have?

Physical Undones

We could all be taking better care of our health. When it comes to your physical health, what do you need to do? Quit smoking, start exercising, stop drinking, avoid fats, slow down, sleep more, take vitamins, run a marathon? What sports or activities would you like to try? Recently, I learned to downhill ski again after being away from the sport for many years. It is an exhilarating feeling to come down the hill at fast speeds. Taking up skiing has given me a renewed appreciation for the winter season as well as helped me stay active. What sport or leisure activity would you like to revisit?

Spiritual Undones

Do you tell the truth? Do your actions match your ethics? Do you keep your agreements and promises? Can others trust you? Do you share important information? Are you connected to your Creator and do you give thanks? Do you spend some time alone each day to reflect and pause? Do you meditate or pray? Did you always want to visit the Holy Land or some important religious shrine? Ask your soul, "What do you need?" To live by the ocean? To paint, to write poetry, to learn to sing? Spiritual undones are subtle, but they come from our deepest longings.

LEARNING TO LET GO

Realize that not all undones have solutions. Sometimes we need to accept what we cannot control, let go and move on. It may be a relationship or a career or a dream. A woman in one of my workshops told me how hard she had tried to nurture a relationship with her alcoholic brother. Every time she visited him, his behavior was erratic, violent, and unpredictable. "I never knew when he was drinking," she said. "I learned that it was almost all the time." When he wouldn't get help, everyone else in the family gave up on him, but not her. She kept visiting him and trying to convince him to get help. One night during an argument, he punched her in the face, breaking her nose and glasses. "That's when I decided," she said. "I had to let go. He was one undone that had to be left alone!"

So many of us have trouble letting go. Monkeys in India are free to roam around in urban areas. In New Delhi, I witnessed an interesting method for capturing monkeys in public places. Trappers would put bamboo cages filled with tiny bananas in a public square, then back off and wait. The monkeys would see the bright yellow bananas and eventually get close to the cage. One or two would stick their hands between the bamboo slats and grab hold of a banana. I learned that once a monkey has a banana in its hand, it won't let go for anything. So imagine this monkey holding onto his banana, but which seems to be attached to this cumbersome cage. He gets upset. He wants his banana, not the cage! He starts jumping up and down, all the while making a huge ruckus because he can't free himself of the cage. All he has to do is let go of the banana, and he'll be free. But he doesn't—won't—can't. And so the trapper comes back and takes him away, banana, cage, and all.

What are you holding on to so tightly that if you could only let go of it, you would free yourself? While most undones have solutions, there are some that we need to walk away from. What do you need to walk away from? What is robbing you of happiness and peace of mind? When I used to counsel couples who were at loggerheads over an issue, I'd tell them, "You can be right, or you can be happy. You choose." What about you? You can hold on or set yourself free. You choose.

EXCUSES WE USE

When we talk of undones, excuses immediately come to mind. Think about your excuses. Here are some of the most common ones:

- **I don't have time.** Let's say you live to be eighty. That means you've got 960 months; 4,160 weeks; 29,200 days; or 700,800 hours. If you're forty, you've got 480 months; 2,080 weeks; 14,600 days; or 350,400 hours left—that is, if you don't get hit by a truck. What you do with this time is your choice. Be proactive. You decide; don't let others decide for you. Do what matters most to you. Make every day count.

- **It's not my fault.** Or "I had no choice" or "It's not my responsibility." When we blame others, we give away our power. We are victims. Studies show that only 3 percent of prison inmates admit accountability for the choices they made that landed them in jail. Some of them, when asked why they are in jail, will answer, "Because my buddy screwed up and I got caught."

- **I keep forgetting.** A variation of this excuse is "I'll put it off, and maybe it'll go away." People who use these excuses are the procrastinators. They need to learn how to activate their action buttons. They need to put the excuses aside and just do it.

- **No one told me.** Or "I didn't have any information" or "I wasn't aware." This is the immature response. When you're a child, you can legitimately use this excuse, but for an adult, it won't wash. Get informed. Find out what you need to know and then do it. Take responsibility for your life.

- **That's just the way I am.** In other words, "I'll never change." These people are choosing to remain closed and ignorant. They are suggesting that they are already complete and that if anyone needs to change, it's the other party. This is their ego speaking, and when your ego speaks, your undones will stay undone. There is no resolution, no healing. Stay open. Entertain the possibility of another way. As a workshop participant once said to me, "Either you're green and growing or ripe and rotten."

Examine these excuses and be honest with yourself. Which ones do you use, and why? You can start tackling some of your undones right now if you're willing to let go of your excuses. We take our lives for granted. We postpone and postpone, thinking we have all the time in the world.

A police officer in my parents' hometown was out doing his job on the last day before his retirement. He had been on the force for thirty years, and he and his wife were now going to take it easy. They were going to do so many things, like take that trip to Fiji that he had always dreamed of. He had pulled over a vehicle with an expired license plate and was standing at the side of the road waiting for the driver to get out his papers, when a passing tractor-trailer struck him down. He died in the hospital three hours later. We never know when our time will be up.

TAKING RISKS BEYOND THE
COMFORT ZONE

**Why are you afraid to take reasonable risks? Are you afraid
of your reputation, afraid of what others think? Ask yourself
these questions: What's to lose? What is the worst that
can happen? Am I content to live the rest of my life this
way? Against a background of death, is this so risky?**

—BRIAN WEISS

In October 1994, the Scandinavian ferry *Estonia* sank off the
coast of Sweden. A violent storm had created an imbalance in its
load. The vehicles that had been lined up in neat rows were
thrown to one side, making the ship lopsided. It didn't take
long for water to pour in and start pulling the vessel down. The
crew knew they were in trouble. They told the passengers that
each of them had a choice to make and they had to do it fast.
The choice was to jump into a tiny boat and hope to be rescued
or to stay on board and risk sinking. There were a thousand
people on board. Most of them looked at the choices and opted
for the comfortable, dry surroundings they were in. A hundred
people had the courage to jump into the unknown, into the raging storm. The ride was rough, but they held on and were eventually rescued. They took the risk and pushed beyond their
fears and their comfort zones, and those hundred brave hearts
are alive today. The rest of them—the nine hundred who stayed
on board—went down with the ship.

You have a choice to make: Do you stretch yourself beyond
your comfort zone or do you stay comfortable but stuck? Do
you take risks and grow? You have probably been told that even
leaving your house is a risk these days. So is getting on a plane or
behind the wheel, and yet we do it. What are some other risks?
Speaking your mind even if it means contradicting someone else,

leaving an abusive relationship, saying no, changing jobs, or moving away. Risk is relative. What is risky for you may not be for me, and vice versa. Think about what risk means to you and what risks you would consider taking.

I have noticed that, for some people, all they have to do is take a risk and their bridge magically appears. Taking risks gives them the faith they need to believe in themselves and to go after whatever it is they want.

Risks must be taken if we want to live fully and participate in this miracle called life. I have been sharing the following poem with audiences for a long time. It paints a disturbing picture of a person who won't take any risks.

To laugh is to risk appearing the fool.
To weep is to risk appearing sentimental.
To reach out for another is to risk involvement.
To expose feelings is to risk exposing our true selves.
To place your ideas, your dreams before the crowd is to risk loss.
To love is to risk not being loved in return.
To live is to risk dying.
To hope is to risk despair.
But risks must be taken because the greatest hazard in life is to risk nothing.
The person who risks nothing, does nothing, has nothing, is nothing.
He may avoid suffering and sorrow, but he simply cannot learn, change, feel, grow, love, live.
Chained by his attitude, he is a slave. He has forfeited freedom.
Only the person who risks is free.
—ANONYMOUS

The paradox is this: All change is uncomfortable, but all growth requires change. To grow, therefore, you must get outside your comfort zone. You must do something different, try something new, activate your action button with courage.

Gandhi said, "Be the change you want to see in the world." In other words, lead! Go first. Be an example. Take action. But how can we do this when so many of us are plagued by our past failures?

STUMBLE FORWARD

It is by going down into the abyss that we recover the treasures of life. Where you stumble, there lies your treasure. The very cave you are afraid to enter turns out to be the source of what you are looking for.

—JOSEPH CAMPBELL

The older I get, the more I realize that life is a series of steps—two steps forward, one step back—and that's okay. When we're young, we're impatient for success and unrealistically think that our progress will be one continuous line going straight up. When we experience setbacks, we become upset and give up. Brave hearts know that failure is part of life, that failure is our ally. Brave hearts learn from failure.

I remember how devastated I was when I learned that I got 50 percent on a calculus exam back in university. It was a pass, but for me it might as well have been zero percent. How could I have failed so miserably? I remember the shame and humiliation I felt. I had stumbled, but it wasn't forward. Stumbling forward would have meant realizing that I had other academic strengths and that I didn't need calculus to fulfill my purpose on earth.

There will be times in your life when you will stumble, experience a setback, lose your job, or fail miserably at a relationship. Instead of feeling bad and becoming depressed, stumble forward. Use the failure as information. Let it grow and transform you. Don't let it rob you of confidence and stop you from taking risks. Let it guide you to define and refine who you are and what your mission is. Since birth, we have been programmed for success. We see failure as a bad thing, something to be ashamed of. (Maybe that explains why some students would rather jump off a ten-story building than go home with their mid-term marks.) And yet failure is part of life. It's not the failure that holds you back; it's your attitude to the failure. How do you react when you stumble? If you learn from it, then you are still moving forward. If you don't learn from it, then it robs you of confidence and energy and you stay stuck.

I like the message in Paul Ferrini's *Love Without Conditions*: "This world is a school, and you have come here to learn. Learning means making mistakes and correcting them. Learning does not mean being right all the time."[3] Mistakes are opportunities to redirect the ship of your life. When you stumble and things don't go your way, think of it as receiving a correction from the divine Mind. "The perception that you are being attacked or punished when things do not go your way is entirely guilt driven," says Ferrini. "Without that guilt, the correction would be received with gratitude . . ."[4] In chapter 4, I talked about the "dark nights of the soul," periods in our lives when we find ourselves in the valley of darkness feeling alone and depressed. Failure can take you there. But this period of trial can be a sort of chicken pox for the soul. Just as childhood diseases like chicken pox are necessary to strengthen the immune system, experiencing failure and the dark nights of the soul are necessary to strengthen your character, commitment, and drive.

SPEAK UP

They came for the Jews, and I said nothing. They came
for the trade unionists, and I said nothing. They came
for the homosexuals, and I said nothing. They came for the
gypsies, and I said nothing. And then they came for me,
and there was no one left to say anything.

—DIETRICH BONHOEFFER

So many of us have been taught to mind our own business, to
not rock the boat, to say nothing. That's one of the reasons why
six million Jews lost their lives. We walk past injustice, closing
our eyes to cruelty, to homelessness, to despair. It's not that we
don't care. It's just that our fears prevent us from doing what's
right. Doing the right thing starts by speaking up!

My client Wayne was depressed. Six months ago, he had an
emotional breakdown at work. He started crying and just
couldn't stop. His sadness was overwhelming. Since then he's
been on antidepressants and is slowly crawling out of his hole.

One morning he called me; he'd had a setback. Wayne is the
youngest of five children. His mother had suffered a stroke, and
he and his siblings rushed to the hospital. The family prayed
together in the chapel. Wayne said it felt good to have all of
them together and talking about childhood memories. "I was
really strong for everyone, especially for my sisters." But as the
days wore on and he was spending his days and nights at his
mother's bedside, the stress began to get to him. He couldn't
sleep. He could feel himself slipping away.

"I feel like I'm going to lose it again," he said to me. After
calming him down, I found out that, besides the lack of sleep
and anxiety about his mother, two key events had robbed him
of his self-respect. One had happened at the hospital when his
sister's know-it-all boyfriend criticized Wayne's family for not

having put their mother in a nursing home. Wayne was terribly disturbed by this attack and the effect it had on everybody. He said nothing, but when he left the hospital, he was angry and shaking. The second event happened the next morning when he told his wife he didn't feel like going to work. Expecting her understanding and support , he was shocked to hear her say, "Well, I hope you're not going to take any more time off." Again, he went silent.

Wayne hates conflict, and he's not alone. Many of us have been brought up to think of conflict as a bad thing. We try to avoid it if possible, and then pay big bucks to intermediaries to solve the conflict for us. When I ask audiences in workshops to write down three undones, unresolved conflicts are always number one on the list. We're programmed from an early age: "Don't make a scene"; "Be nice"; "Don't say anything." All this programming has collectively muzzled us. We shut up, put up with, keep quiet, give in, and swallow our truth—and slowly, slowly we say goodbye to our self-respect.

It takes courage to speak up. Depending on how much self-confidence we have at any one time, many of us are not prepared to take the risk. "If I tell my boss what I truly think, I may be out of a job." "If I speak up at this family gathering, then everybody will be upset." "If I tell my friend what I think, maybe she won't like me anymore or judge me unfairly." Sometimes, when there are intense emotions, it's okay to take a time-out and say nothing. It's okay to postpone speaking up, but not for long! The rule is seven days—if you don't address the conflict by then, chances are you never will. Sure, there are times we let things slide or turn a blind eye, and that's okay. But if it becomes a habit and you're consistently silent while inside you're screaming, then you need to pay attention.

Using our voices and speaking up is our birthright, but it is risky. If we don't risk it, though, we stay victimized. I don't have a large build, but I have always been able to use my voice to protect myself and those I love. When I was a kid, I used my voice to rescue my younger brother from bullies. John, who is three years younger than me, had a lisp, wore thick glasses, and walked pigeon-toed. He was an easy target for abuse. I was smaller than the bullies and some of them were older than me, but the fury in my voice scared them away. They knew better than to mess with big sister.

Many people in my workshops tell me they're too afraid to speak up at work. You've probably seen this scenario. No one speaks up at general meetings, but afterwards in the halls, the bathrooms, and the cafeteria, everyone has an opinion. You don't have to scream and shout. Be assertive, not aggressive. Assertive people are tough on issues, but soft on people. They're not belligerent or rude, but they do ask to be heard.

Words can be powerful, but it's how you use them that's important. It's your tone of voice and your mannerisms. If you open your mouth but sound tentative, people will not listen to you. Act confident. Practice speaking up with a friend or in front of a mirror if you have to. Is there someone in your life with whom you need to exchange words? When we don't speak up, we lose self-respect and nerve. It happens little by little, like a drip on a rock, eventually eroding who we are and what we stand for. Inevitably, we end up paying a price. Depending on your chemistry, your unspoken truth will go to either your reservoir of anger or your reservoir of sadness. If it goes to your reservoir of anger, then eventually, it will get full, and you'll explode. If it goes to your reservoir of sadness, you shut down and eventually become depressed.

That's what happened with Wayne. We are complex, inter-connected, spiritual beings. When we swallow our truth and keep our thoughts and feelings to ourselves, we are denying a part of who we are. We push our authentic Self further and further away until we no longer know who we are. It's no wonder that so many adults in mid-life have an identity crisis. Remember Eleanor Roosevelt's empowering message: "No one can make you feel inferior without your consent." Speak up. Try it once and notice the difference. That will give you the confidence to do it again. Exercise your voice. Feel the fear, but open your mouth anyway.

PLAY THE GAME OFFENSIVELY

I've missed more than 9,000 shots in my career. I've lost almost 300 games. Twenty-six times I've been trusted to take the game winning shot and missed. I've failed over and over and over again in my life. And that is why I succeed.

—MICHAEL JORDAN

My son Jasper plays soccer. I asked his coach one season if Jasper could try playing forward. He had scored a goal and talked about wanting to try a different position besides defense. His coach wasn't receptive to the idea because, he told me, "I need Jasper mid-field. He doesn't let anything get by." While that was a nice compliment, I thought it odd that the coach's primary concern was protecting the net rather than scoring goals.

It occurred to me that there are people who play the game of life that way. If you play defensively, you're motivated by fear—fear that someone else might get the job, someone might beat you to the punch, someone else might be better than you—so you're constantly on the alert and worried that someone might take something away. Consequently, you pour all your resources into defending your net and waiting for the action to come to you. People like that never take risks, because they're too focused on protecting their net. They never get past mid-field.

If, on the other hand, you play the game of life offensively, you go for the ball. You lead; you take risks. You're a brave heart. You're not afraid to take the ball and run with it. That doesn't mean that you never act defensively and it doesn't mean that you win all the time; it just means that you pour more energy into taking shots on goal than defending your net. The Brazilian soccer team plays that way. They're passionate and fearless. They go for the net. They don't always win, but they play the most exciting, entertaining soccer, and to me that's what it's all about. All of us need to be playing an exciting game of life. How about you? Do you play life offensively or defensively? Are you passionate about scoring goals or intent on protecting your net? Every day you have a choice as to how you will play in the arena of life. You can play it safe, or you can take a risk.

CHALLENGE YOUR MENTAL MAPS

**Each of us tends to think we see things as they are,
that we are objective. But this is not the case.
We see the world, not as it is, but as we are—
or as we are conditioned to see it.**

—STEPHEN COVEY

I had just boarded an airplane when I noticed a man in first class who had pinned his silk tie to his shirt with those huge safety pins you use for diapers. The tie was all bunched up, and it looked ridiculous. Confused, I scanned his face. "Is he one of those idiot savant types who can multiply ten-digit numbers in his head but not dress himself?" I wondered. "Why didn't anyone check him out before he left the house this morning? Here he is traveling out of town in first class, looking like that. Poor man." I looked around to see if anyone else had noticed him, but people seemed indifferent. "Too polite, or too stressed out," I thought, and then as I moved up a few paces, I experienced a paradigm shift. The man's tie was holding up his arm, which was in a cast. I hadn't been able to see the full picture from where I had been standing before. I felt silly, but the incident made me think about how often we argue for our point of view when we don't have all the facts. Sometimes all we have to do is move up and look a little closer, and a different truth will be revealed to us.

Our core beliefs or thoughts form a screen through which we experience the world. These are our mental maps, our filters or paradigms. We don't usually allow information that is inconsistent with our beliefs to seep through our filters. Thomas Kuhn found this to be the case even with scientists. In his book *The Structure of Scientific Revolutions,* Kuhn argued that only data that agrees with the scientist's paradigms—that is, his world view—are allowed to filter through. For us to grow, we must be open to seeing the world differently. We must try on a different pair of glasses. When we do this, we experience an *aha!*—a moment of illumination or a paradigm shift.

Moments of illumination will not come if we are arrogant or too certain about our beliefs. Certainty keeps us locked into old paradigms. Where would we be today without discoveries and inventions such as electricity, the theory of relativity, airplanes, the radio, and the microchip? It takes courage to challenge our mental maps, to see the world from a different angle, to take off our blinders. Creativity happens when we can step beyond the norm and ask a different question. But to do this we need to be brave hearts. Perhaps we need to step outside our heads and see with the eyes of the heart. What area of your life needs a shake?

A few years ago I hired a young woman to help me with administration. Lori was also working at another part-time job, as well as taking evening courses. Her days were full, yet every time she met one of her relatives, she'd walk away feeling "less than" because she did not have that much sought after full-time permanent job. "What if you told them you're a consultant?" I suggested to her one day. "And that you already have two major clients!"

Her eyes lit up. "I'll try it," she said. Her relatives were impressed, and Lori walked away feeling empowered and in charge of her destiny. And all she had done was challenge her own mental map of how she earned a living, by reinterpreting her work experience.

To be able to challenge our mental maps, we need to become aware of the way we perceive the world. What perspective do we come from? My grandmother, whom I called "Nonna," lived in a small town in southern Italy for most of her life. She didn't do much traveling, because she never left the side of her handicapped daughter, Barbarella. You can imagine the excitement when her son, my Uncle Jimmy, who was visiting from Australia, proposed they go to Foggia to visit the shrine of the Madonna. In the car on the way home, Nonna gazed at the beautiful sunset and became pensive. Foggia was less than two hours by car from her home, but she turned to Uncle Jimmy and said, "*Mamma mia, come e grande questo mondo,*" which means "Oh my gosh, this world is so big!"

It was an innocent remark from a woman who had led a simple life, but it charged up my uncle. "What would you think of the world if you had spent thirty-five hours on a plane?" he asked her. How is it that two people can share an experience yet feel such different things? It's because, as the Talmud says, "We do not see the world as it is; we see the world as we are."

In *Everyday Soul: Awakening the Spirit in Daily Life,* Bradford Keeney talks about an experiment carried out by the biologist John Lilly. Lilly recorded the word "cogitate" on a tape over and over again. Later, when people listened to the tape, they heard more than two thousand different words and word combinations, for example, agitate, arbitrate, candidate, computate, stop the tape, can't you stay, conscious state, count to ten, cut a steak, got a date, got to take, gurgitate, etc. What you hear depends on who you are and what mental maps you have. Keeney writes, "Life itself is like an endless tape that repeats the same sound. What we hear, see, and feel are therefore statements about our participation in life rather than any objective representation of what is really happening to us."[5]

There's a story I love about a young man driving down a country road. He's got the top down on his convertible, the sun is shining, and he's enjoying all the wonderful twists and turns in the road. Suddenly, another car comes careening around the bend and nearly hits him. As it passes him, the driver sticks her head out the window and yells, "Pig!" Indignant, the young man thinks, "How dare she call me a pig? She's the one who can't drive." He accelerates around the bend and runs straight into the pig.

Sometimes we think the world is one way when it's not. Then the truth slaps us in the face, and we must relinquish old paradigms. But that's how we grow; that's how we shed our old skin and make way for the new. What area of your life needs to be perceived differently? Who has been yelling "pig" at you? What possibilities and opportunities have been waiting for you to see them? Which mental maps have been preventing you from crossing your bridge?

ACT AS IF YOU KNOW

**Act as if you are and you will draw it to you.
What you act as if you are you become.**

—NEALE DONALD WALSCH

At a workshop I once attended, the instructor used the principle of "act as if you know" when people got stuck and asked him for answers. He was teaching a visualization technique that involved imagining your future. A few people felt they couldn't do that and so, frustrated, they asked the instructor for the right answer. He calmly asked them one by one, "Well, what do you think?"

The reply would come, "I don't know. That's why I'm asking you."

And he'd say, "Well, I know you don't know, but if you *did* know, what would the answer be?" Instantly, they'd have an answer.

"Well, that's your answer then," he'd say, and then he'd move on to the next person.

As soon as each person experienced this amazing shift they would sit back and grin. "Hey," they seemed to be saying, "I did have the answer." When the light bulb went on for others, their faces would flush with embarrassment, as if to say, "That's it? It's that simple?"

It was absolutely magical to watch. We all have the answers deep inside us, but sometimes we need someone skilled to pull them out. Throughout the weekend, any time someone got stuck he'd use the same technique: "I know you don't know, but if you *did* know, what would the answer be?"

Brilliant. It got so that, as soon as a question was asked, the rest of us would start to recite, "I know you don't know, but . . ." By the end of the weekend, we realized that there was no such thing as not knowing who we were. If we had forgotten, we just had to be reminded. The truth is always there inside of us.

The Greek philosopher Plato wrote about this nearly two thousand years ago. His theory was that all knowledge is remembered—that knowledge precedes experience and that everything we seek to know is already within us. Modern-day philosophers are saying the same thing. Go within, find your authentic Self, tap into your inner wisdom, listen to your higher Self.

The next time you're faced with a difficult decision or uncertainty, act as if you already know. This is another way to activate your action button or give yourself the courage you need to take action. Ask yourself:

- I know I don't know what to do in this situation, but if I did know, what would I do?
- I know I don't know what to say, but if I did know, what would I say?
- I know I don't have an answer, but if I did have the answer, what would it be?

This is a powerful technique for getting in touch with your intuition, your sacred Self, and your higher Wisdom.

Another way to take action, even when you feel afraid and unsure of yourself, is to act as if you belong. I was fresh out of school and looking for work, and I knew that no one at the Canadian Broadcasting Corporation was hiring because of a recent, much publicized hiring freeze. I knew that if I was going to get into the celebrated CBC, I would need to make an impression. So I turned up in my best suit, straightened my back, and walked past the parking attendants and the security guards, up the elevator, past the receptionist, and right into the office of the executive producer of CBC TV News. No one challenged me. No one asked for my ID. I just walked in. The executive producer was awestruck. Several times he asked me how I had managed to get into his office.

"I don't know, I just walked in," I replied.

He shook his head in disbelief. "But you don't have any ID. How did you get past security?"

I shrugged. "I just walked in," I said.

He told me that without any broadcasting experience I would find television too difficult a medium. "Learn radio first. In a few years, you can try TV." He was so impressed by my nerve that he sent me to his colleague at CBC Radio News. I got an entry-level position and stayed with CBC for five years, working as a reporter, editor, and producer. I know that my foot in the door there was that I had acted as if I already belonged.

To take that first step over your bridge you may need to act as if you know, act as if you belong, or act as if you have already succeeded in crossing the bridge, even if you're scared to death on the inside. Remember to ask yourself, "What's the worst thing that could happen to me?" Naming your worst fear is often the first step in relinquishing its power over you. Whether it's starting your own business, quitting your job, going back to school, or declaring your love, you must start taking action—whether the fear is in your knees, your chest, or your stomach. If your faith is weak and you don't believe you can do it, *act* as if you can do it, and watch your faith grow. You might just surprise yourself.

DON'T BE ATTACHED TO OUTCOME

Instead of worrying about specific outcomes and results, just do the right thing.

—BRIAN WEISS

Anthropologist Angeles Arrien, in her book *The Four-Fold Way*, cites four principles for living: (1) show up, (2) pay attention, (3) tell the truth, and (4) don't be attached to outcome.[6] Although all four principles are challenging, I have discovered that most people find the fourth principle the most difficult.

As humans, one of our greatest faults is our overwhelming need to know the outcome. We are preoccupied with end results, and this preoccupation creates much of our malaise. Consequently, many of us lead conditional lives. "I'll love you if you love me"; "I'll give you this if you give me that"; "I'll be happy if everything goes my way." So we stop loving, stop risking, and stop living because we're too attached to the results. We have come to care more about the score than the game, more about the destination than the journey, more about the marks than the learning, more about the answer than the question. We need to take action, because it's the right thing to do. We need to show our love to the world, give away our gifts, try new things, take risks, and not worry about what others will think or say. Our actions can have both good and bad results; positive or negative outcomes. Attachment to the results can make us fearful, and fear prevents us from taking action, from walking across the bridge.

Imagine yourself vulnerable, soft, and loving—and pouring out that love to someone who's ungrateful and callous. Perhaps you remember a time when you made a fuss over a friend's birthday and then he or she forgot yours. We've all suffered disappointments. Those disappointments fuel our inability to live rule number 4. "Hope is fine," says Brian Weiss in his *Messages from the Masters*. "Expectation is not, because when expectation is present, disappointment is always lurking by."[7] "Don't be attached to outcome" means "do it anyway." Show your love, try out for the team, apply for the job, start that business, change careers, travel to Africa, dream big—live.

In the previous section, I told you to act as if you are, to expect success and it will come to you. Now I'm telling you not to have any expectations. Let me explain. I think it's natural to have expectations, but too often we expect great things from others but not from ourselves. Expecting the bridge to be there when you cross it is an act of faith—faith in your abilities. Whether others give you something in return for what you've given them is out of your control. Don't set yourself up for disappointment. You can't control others, just yourself.

MAKE DECISIONS

Move in the wind. Your life is a dance.
Your choice is a simple one. You can dance or not.
—PAUL FERRINI

Are you one of those people who can't make decisions? The ones who sit on the fence and wait for someone to push them off? Making a decision is a courageous move. That's because you must take responsibility for your decisions, and often we are too immature to accept the consequences. But your soul wants you to make decisions, because when you choose to move in the wind, you are expressing who you are. Making decisions tells the world who you are. Do I live in the country or in the city? Do I drive or take transit? Do I paint my apartment teal or orange? Do I rent or own? We make decisions every day. Do I eat chicken or pasta? Do I stop for this amber light or drive through? To live from your authentic place, you need to embrace decision making.

It's better to follow your own path, make a mistake, and learn from it, than to make no decision at all and coast, or worse, wait for someone else to decide your destiny. When you make decisions, you come face-to-face with fear. Regardless of the outcome or whether it's a good or bad decision, when we make a decision, we grow. We can never know the result of an exam before we take it, just as we can never know if a choice is right before it is made. That's why decisions can be risks. Sometimes we make simple decisions like "It's time to go to bed." That is not a risk. I'm talking about life decisions: Do I marry him? Do I leave this job? Do I speak my mind? Do I move to where my heart is calling me? Do I step across the bridge?

If we don't make the decisions that need to be made, we end up postponing our lives forever. We're just buying time. Have you heard these? "I'll do it when I get a job." "I'll do it after we have kids." "I'll do it when we move to our new house." "I'll do it when the kids grow up." "I'll do it when the kids move away." Get the picture? What's life without courage, growth, choice, even if that choice includes error? The path of life will have potholes, but so what? It doesn't prevent you from jumping over them. You may fall and skin your knees or your pride, but that's how we learn. That's the way it's always been. We get up and try again. We stumble forward. We must take that risk in order to participate fully in the human experience. I *encourage* you not to wait for someone else to make your decisions. Be a brave heart and decide!

Reflections and Helpful Exercises:

1. Carpe Diem Exercise

If I were to ask you to complete the following sentence, how would you finish it? "If there were no obstacles in my life, some day I would . . ."

If there were no obstacles in your life (for example, if you had enough money, time, and courage), what would you do? Then make a list of reasons why you have not seized the day yet. Look at those reasons. Are they really obstacles, or does your perception need to change? Choose one thing you'd like to focus on and then write an action plan (see the exercise on setting goals at the end of chapter 3). In other words, ask yourself what action steps you need to take in order to make this happen. These adventures and dreams are waiting for you on the other side of the bridge. They are all possible. All you need to do is to seize the day and *just do it!*

2. Meditation on Fear

To help clients move beyond their fear, I use this exercise to make them aware of how fear may show up in their bodies and be preventing them from taking the step.

Get relaxed.

Standing indoors or out, focus on your breath. With each inhalation and exhalation, feel your body relaxing. Concentrate on your breath for a few minutes and feel your shoulders—your whole body, in fact—sinking deeper towards the ground.

Focus on a desire.

Close your eyes and think of something you want, something that is waiting for you on the other side of the bridge—your heart's desire. It can be a tangible goal or something internal, like feeling more confident or more courageous. Imagine your life with this desire fulfilled. What does it look like and feel like to have this desire fulfilled? Use all of your senses. Make it vivid and colorful.

Start moving.

Now open your eyes and pick a spot right in front of you at least ten feet away. It may be the trunk of a tree in your backyard or the door to your bathroom or the fireplace or the fence. Focus on this place and imagine that it represents what you want, the desire you have been concentrating on. Begin moving towards it, taking note of how your body is feeling. If fear comes up, name it and identify its location and how it is affecting you. Don't try to ignore it or push it away or pretend it doesn't exist. Befriend it. But keep moving your feet towards your desire. If you have to pause, that's okay, but don't rush. Just stay with what you are feeling. Keep the vision of your desire alive in your mind. This will allow you to keep moving despite the uncomfortable feelings you may be experiencing.

3. Ask "Did Anyone Die?"

I recently reconnected with someone I hadn't seen in twenty-five years. Debbie and I were best friends in elementary school. She showed up at one of my lectures, which had been advertised in her city's newspaper. It was great to see her again. In a letter she wrote to me afterwards, she told me that she and her husband had lost their first baby because it had a heart defect. The experience had changed them and helped them to prioritize what was most important in their lives. Now when there are upsets in the family or one of them is having a personal crisis, they'll ask, "Did anyone die?" It helps them focus on the essentials.

I think we could all ask this question more often when the world is crumbling at our feet and we are gripped by fear. It's similar to that other great question, "What's the worst that can happen?" For most people, the worst that can happen is death, and death is rarely the outcome of so much that we fear. It's not death that prevents us from walking across the bridge, it's Fantasized Events that Appear Real. Isn't that what the letters in FEAR represent? These questions—"Did anyone die?" and "What's the worst that can happen?"—express the sentiment that even though our fear appears to engulf us at times, it can be put into perspective. Fear may be the last frontier, but it doesn't have to run your life. To have courage is to have heart and hope, and to move your life forward, despite the uncomfortable feelings.

Epilogue

The experience of being loved by the ultimate Mystery banishes every fear. It is as if God planted a great big kiss in the middle of our Spirit and all the wounds, doubts, and guilt feelings were all healed at the same moment.

—FATHER THOMAS KEATING

A few years ago, I came to the conclusion that teaching people secular faith—that is, helping them find the confidence and faith in themselves through workshops, therapy, coaching, or other psychological modalities—cannot lead to true empowerment unless they go inward and connect to their Spirit or God Essence. That's because many of our problems stem not from a psychological root, but from a spiritual root. For years people have been sent to psychiatrists, psychologists, and psychoanalysts to have their pathologies labeled and fixed. In all fairness, clinical psychology has tried to help, but it has missed the mark with many people. I think that's because the practice of psychology doesn't allow people the flexibility to discover their own spirituality and connect with the Great Spirit that dwells

Grace Cirocco

inside each of us. We are mind, body, heart, and Spirit, and slowly we are realizing that we need a holistic approach to healing. Psychology might get you across the bridge, but in my opinion, it cannot give you lasting peace, joy, and fulfillment.

The field of spiritual psychology is quickly emerging to quench some of the thirst. Every day I meet people who are looking for "spiritual answers"—spiritual warriors and goddesses embarking on their private journeys—a path that will take them face-to-face with their inner demons, their worst fears, and their greatest dreams. This community of Light Seekers is expanding around the world. Some would say that we're in the midst of the Great Spiritual Awakening; others might call it a spiritual revolution. However we label this movement towards health, wholeness, and Spirit, I know that the personal growth of the individual is the building block for the growth of the organization, the family, and the community at large. When we work at becoming better versions of ourselves, we inspire others to do the same. When we heal ourselves, we heal the planet and together we raise the vibrational energy of the Universe.

I began this book with the question "Who are you?" and I am ending it by reminding you that who you are is a spiritual being having a human experience. Whatever you want to do, whoever you want to be, recognize first that you are a fragment of the Divine Creator, God, the Universe (this energy source goes by many names). I call it Spirit.

Connect to Spirit and you connect to your higher Self—the part of you that has dreams and desires to take the step and cross the bridge towards endless possibilities. Connect to Spirit and you connect to your Divinity—that part of you that is beautiful, pure, and eternal. And finally, connect to Spirit, and you will activate the brave heart that lives inside you.

246

Everything that happens to you, whether positive or negative, is necessary for your spiritual evolution. Stop fighting yourself. Stop feeling so alone. We're not really alone. Spirit is there in the form of angels, guides, and intuition. It has always been there, guiding you, nurturing you, and holding your hand. May your Spirit continue to be your beacon of Light as you take your step.

The first visit to the moon happened more than thirty years ago, and yet—as I've heard experts say—Neil Armstrong's footprints are still there today. That's because there's no weather on the moon—no rain, no wind, no snow to wear them away. Imagine! Well, one day it will be your time to go. What "footprints" will you leave behind? How do you want to be remembered? Decide today how you want to make a difference in the world. What gifts and talents, hopes and dreams are still lying dormant inside you? It is time for you to be, do, and have all that your heart desires. Live authentically, passionately, and courageously! Reach for those luminous places not only within yourself, but in others, so that together we can create a better world.

Knowledge without action is wasted. Faith without action is not faith. And life without action is unlived. Take your step, dance across your bridge, and make the rest of your life truly extraordinary.

GRACE CIROCCO

End Notes

Chapter 1: Honor Your Authentic Self

1 Mark Albion, *Making a Life, Making a Living* (New York: Warner Books, 2000), 9.
2 Georgia Witkin, *The Female Stress Syndrome* (New York: Newmarket Press, 1991) and *The Male Stress Syndrome* (New York: Newmarket Press, 1996).
3 Robin Norwood, *Why Me, Why This, Why Now?* (Toronto: McClelland & Stewart, 1994), 12.
4 Caroline Myss, *Why People Don't Heal and How They Can* (New York: Three Rivers Press, 1997), 12.
5 Oriah Mountain Dreamer, *The Invitation* (San Francisco: HarperSanFrancisco, 1999), 1.
6 Nag Hammadi Codices 11.33.18–21.

Chapter 2: Discover Your Destiny

1 Stephen Covey, *The Seven Habits of Highly Effective People* (New York: Simon & Schuster, 1989), 108.
2 Mitch Albom, *Tuesdays with Morrie* (New York: Doubleday, 1997), 82.

Chapter 3: Awaken Your Passion

1 Sarah Ban Breathnach, "A Gift for Giving," *People* (September 22, 1997): 101–102.

2 Marianne Williamson, *A Woman's Worth* (New York: Random House, 1993), 14.
3 Og Mandino, *The Greatest Miracle in the World* (New York: Bantam Books, 1975), 91.
4 Barbara De Angelis, *Passion* (New York: Delacorte Press, 1998), 20.
5 *The Essential Rumi*, Coleman Barks, trans. (New York: HarperCollins, 1995), 105.
6 Robert Fritz, *The Path of Least Resistance*, quoted in Barbara J.   1
   Braham, *Finding Your Purpose* (Menlo Park, CA: Crisp Publications, 1991), 4.
7 Braham, 5.
8 Brian Weiss, *Messages from the Masters: Tapping into the Power of Love* (New York: Warner Books, 2000), 108–9.
9 Sam Keen, *The Passionate Life* (San Francisco: HarperSanFrancisco, 1992), 254.
10 Sarah Ban Breathnach, *Something More* (New York: Warner Books, 1998), 156.
11 Diane Ackerman, *A Natural History of the Senses*, quoted in *O* magazine, "Diane Sawyer Shares a Great Read" (September 2000), 274.

Chapter 4: Heal Your Past

1 Gabriele Rico, *Pain and Possibility* (New York: Jeremy P. Tarcher/Perigee Books, 1991), viii.
2 Thomas Moore, *Care of the Soul* (New York: Harper Perennial, 1992), 136.
3 Debbie Ford, *The Dark Side of the Light Chasers* (New York: Riverhead Books, 1998), 24–25.
4 David Whyte, *The Heart Aroused* (New York: Currency Doubleday, 1994), 109.
5 Joan Borysenko, *Fire in the Soul: A New Psychology of Spiritual Optimism* (New York: Warner Books, 1994), 9 and 58.
6 Norman Cousins, quoted in Rico, 7.
7 Alice Miller, *The Drama of the Gifted Child* (New York: Basic Books, 1994), 35.

Chapter 5: Esteem Your Self

1 Nathaniel Branden, *The Power of Self-Esteem* (New York: Health Communications, 1992), viii.
2 Mandino, 97.
3 Dannion Brinkley, "We are All Great, Awesome, Powerful, Spiritual Beings," *Experiencing the Soul*, Eliot Jay Rosen, ed. (Carlsbad, CA: Hay House, 1998), 103.

End Notes

4 Nag Hammadi Codices 11.45.29–33.

5 John K. Williams, *The Knack of Using Your Subconscious Mind* (New Jersey: Prentice-Hall, 1980), 27.

6 Neale Donald Walsch, *Conversations with God Book 3* (Hampton Roads Publishing Company, 1998), 61.

7 Ibid., 60.

8 All examples from Williams.

9 Williams, 26.

10 See Thomas Verny, *The Secret Life of the Unborn Child* (Toronto: Collins, 1981).

11 In Elaine Dembe, *Use the Good Dishes: Finding Joy in Everyday Life* (Toronto: Macmillan, 2000), 85.

Chapter 6: Activate Your Courage

1 Oriah Mountain Dreamer, *The Invitation* (San Francisco: HarperSanFrancisco, 1999), 91.

2 Theodore Roosevelt, "Citizenship in a Republic," speech delivered at Sorbonne, Paris, April 23, 1910 (U.S. History Interactive 1999, Theodore Roosevelt Quotations).

3 Paul Ferrini, *Love Without Conditions* (Greenfield, MA: Heartways Press, 1994), 49.

4 Ferrini, 33.

5 Bradford Keeney, *Everyday Soul: Awakening the Spirit in Daily Life* (New York: Riverhead Books, 1996), 30.

6 Angeles Arrien, *The Four-Fold Way* (New York: HarperCollins, 1993), 7–8.

7 Weiss, 101.

Dear friends,

Thank you for taking the step and adding this book to your library. We hope it will give you encouragement and inspiration as you continue to actualize your highest ideals for your life.

If you would like to hire Grace Cirocco as a keynote speaker at an upcoming conference or event, please e-mail info@gracecirocco.com.

If you would like more information on Grace Cirocco, please visit www.gracecirocco.com.

If you would like more information on Grace's retreats and programs for women, visit www.goddessgrowth.com.